Grieving Well

Praise for *Grieving Well*

Grieving Well arrives at the ideal time when the world truly needs its message. Grief is something we all must face. With stories from others who've dealt with it, we realize in our shared humanity that we are not alone. Others are dealing with life challenges, too, and their experiences and stories can help us if we are open-minded and humble ourselves to receive it.

Tony Rubleski, best-selling author, speaker, and coach, founder of Mind Capture Group

While I've learned about grief and grace through dozens of natural disasters around the world, it's not something I had read about. In *Grieving Well,* Terri and Janet cover the critical topic of grief in a graceful way that is helpful for everyone, everywhere.

Ginger Zee, chief meteorologist, managing editor Climate Unit, ABC News

My profession—and frankly, my family dynamic for that matter—has always kept me in a position of "outward happiness." In other words, "grin and bear it." *Grieving Well* gives actual tools on how to stand in grief. The chapter on a timeline made me hold my hand over my heart as I read it. *It's OKAY to grieve. A timeline is absurd . . .* these words are comforting. Sometimes, we need permission to feel a certain way. Terri and Janet not only give us permission but have held our hands and walked us through pain, sadness, and grieving. *Grieving Well* will be at the top of my gift list for friends and family for years to come.

Michelle McKormick, radio host, WLAV Grand Rapids, radio talent coach, Cumulus Media

Grieving Well is a call to action, a reminder that we will live and die. The art of grieving is part of our journey. *Grieving Well* offers preparation through spiritual guidance and personal testimonies that will be part of my required reading, as should be for all.

Shelley Irwin, host of the WGVU Morning Show, NPR, Grand Rapids, Michigan

Over the last fifteen years of ministry, I have observed grief take many forms. The journey through loss is often disorienting and devastatingly lonely. *Grieving Well* navigates this journey with grace and compassion, and includes a beautiful variety of stories told by those who have personally experienced loss. It is both practical and profound . . . and most importantly, it is a reminder that in our darkest moments, we are not alone. HIGHLY RECOMMENDED!

Rev. Tim Wilson, lead pastor, South Harbor Church

Though grief is universal it can often feel isolating. *Grieving Well* is full of heartwarming and heart-mending essays that will show you are not alone.

Tracy Brogan Books, Amazon, *Wall Street Journal,* and *USA Today* bestselling author

We can't escape this truth: Grief is a part of life but still terribly hard. Part resource, part mini-memoir, and part devotional, *Grieving Well* is the compilation of the authors' expertise and contributors' stories, meant to connect us all through hope. After all, one of the deepest comforts we can experience is knowing we are not alone in our grief. Kudos to all who braved their grief, chose vulnerability, and openly shared their stories. *Grieving Well* serves as a hug for everyone who reads it.

Cortney Donelson, author, speaker, and founder of vocem LLC

Larry and I hope and pray that *Grieving Well* touches the hearts and souls of those walking the grief journey. We are confident that what you find in *Grieving Well* is what we have known about Faith Hospice for so many years. Thank you, Faith Hospice Bereavement for sharing your expertise and your loving methods to help so many who are hurting.

Nancy Erhardt, member, Founding Faith Hospice Board

Terri DeBoer and Janet Jaymin have written a "down to earth" map for the grieving process, realizing there is no normal grief journey. Grief is an individualized journey but not one that needs to be traveled alone. *Grieving Well* is a wonderful compilation of facts, tips, and personal stories.

Mina Breuker, former president & CEO, Faith Hospice

Grieving Well, a beautiful book on navigating the seasons of grief and loss will speak to your heart in many ways. It is a resource that you will come back to time and again for insight and support. Having worked with Janet over the years, I have witnessed her care for so many families, including my own. I know first-hand that the words in *Grieving Well* will be a balm to tired and hurting souls, and that by learning to grieve well, we will in turn find the tools to live well even through our loss.

Amy Van Andel, patient advocate and former hospice nurse

Janet Jaymin is an amazing and qualified healthcare professional who lovingly walks beside the bereaved she serves. The stigma I perceived of not needing a therapist was broken when I began working through my grief with Janet as my grief counselor. Not only are Janet's intellectual and clinical skills wonderful, but she also gently and compassionately helped me explore, understand, and process the feelings and pain associated with losing my dear wife, Cathy. Janet helped me get to the other side of grief. I am grateful that *Grieving Well* will provide a piece of Janet's talents with others.

Carl Paganelli, NFL official, Faith Hospice family

Grieving Well

A Healing Journey
through the Season of Grief

Terri DeBoer
& Janet Jaymin

NASHVILLE

NEW YORK • LONDON • MELBOURNE • VANCOUVER

Grieving Well

A Healing Journey Through the Season of Grief

Published in New York, New York, by Morgan James Publishing. Morgan James is a trademark of Morgan James, LLC. www.MorganJamesPublishing.com

Proudly distributed by Ingram Publisher Services.

Morgan James BOGO™

A **FREE** ebook edition is available for you or a friend with the purchase of this print book.

CLEARLY SIGN YOUR NAME ABOVE

Instructions to claim your free ebook edition:
1. Visit MorganJamesBOGO.com
2. Sign your name CLEARLY in the space above
3. Complete the form and submit a photo of this entire page
4. You or your friend can download the ebook to your preferred device

ISBN 9781631959592 paperback
ISBN 9781631959608 ebook
Library of Congress Control Number:
2022936700

Cover and Interior Design by:
Chris Treccani
www.3dogcreative.net

Morgan James PUBLISHING **Builds** with... **Habitat for Humanity** Peninsula and Greater Williamsburg

Morgan James is a proud partner of Habitat for Humanity Peninsula and Greater Williamsburg. Partners in building since 2006.

Get involved today! Visit MorganJamesPublishing.com/giving-back

To those who are on a personal journey of grief or supporting someone who is suffering a loss. May *Grieving Well* serve as a source of comfort and hope in the search for peace.

Table Of Contents

Acknowledgments

To the "angels on earth" who work at Faith Hospice, providing loving, compassionate care for those approaching the end of life

To Rene Wheaton, executive vice president of Faith Hospice, for her support and vision for the impact of this project.

To Tammy Sue Veldkamp, Faith Hospice executive director, for her perennial leadership.

To the Board members and leadership (past and present) of Faith Hospice whose vision has shaped the excellent quality of care for residents and their families.

To Gerilyn May for using her incredible organizational and copyediting skills to develop the rich content in this book, and for sharing her own personal journey of grief.

To David Hancock and the team at Morgan James Publishing for your partnership in bringing this book to readers. A special thank you to Author Relations Manager Shannon Peters.

To Tom Dean and A Drop Of Ink for seeing the value of this important message and guiding the team through the publication process.

To Cortney Donelson for her guidance, perspective, and heart for helping those who are hurting; her editorial and technical expertise have been critical in shaping this material.

To those special contributors who bravely shared their personal and painful stories of grief; please know your honesty will provide hope and comfort to countless people you will never meet.

Our greatest gratitude is for the peace and hope through all seasons of life that comes from a relationship with Jesus Christ and our amazing Heavenly Father, and the promise of eternal life in Him.

To our loved ones that we have lost, we are grateful for enduring memories. They will never be forgotten.

From Janet Jaymin

There are not enough words to express my thankfulness to my co-author, Terri DeBoer, for taking a vision and making it come to fruition. I thank you for walking alongside me, guiding the process of writing this book together—with no doubt only grace and encouragement.

Thank you to my wonderful Faith Hospice bereavement team: Julie Ball, Jen Gruppen, and Gail Hengeveld. You have supported me with joyful enthusiasm and those words do not do justice to the kindness and great generosity you have provided, day in and day out.

Thank you, Faith Hospice leadership team—your support has been unwavering.

My big sisters, Judy and Cindy, thank you for the unconditional love.

To my parents, who taught me that Kindness, Compassion, and Love are the true meaning of Life and God is always faithful.

From Terri DeBoer

My deepest appreciation to my co-author, Janet Jaymin, for identifying my own "journey of grief" in the "Empty Nest" transition and planting the creative seed for *Grieving Well*. I'm grateful for Janet's countless hours of reflection and energy in making difficult concepts easy to understand and so relatable.

Foreword

. . . and the God of all comfort, who comforts us in all our troubles, so that we can comfort those in any trouble with the comfort we ourselves receive from God.

2 Corinthians 1:3b–4

After working in the hospice industry for more than twenty-five years, I have witnessed hundreds of families dealing with loss in various ways. Understanding how to offer help and comfort to those experiencing loss is a special gift.

Terri DeBoer and Janet Jaymin come from two different perspectives yet have been able to meld their perspectives in an amazing way. Both have a focus on helping people respond to life's challenges, either dealing with the ever-changing Michigan weather or helping those who have experienced various losses in their life. The goal of this book is to help the reader walk through their own grief journey and learn that even though we all experience grief differently, we are never alone.

My prayer is for *Grieving Well* to serve as a personal guidebook for those who are hurting after suffering a loss. May the words and stories contained in these pages provide an opportunity to learn about grief and may the personal stories shared by the brave individuals provide inspiration, perspective, and hope.

Finally, may the specially-written devotions serve as a guide for finding a deeper understanding of the comfort, hope, and peace that is contained in God's Word.

I sincerely hope you find this book as meaningful as I did.

René Wheaton
Executive Vice President
Faith Hospice

Preface

As I was preparing to release my first book in the fall of 2021, I was invited into a meeting with the team at Faith Hospice to discuss my possible role as a speaker for a fundraising event they were planning. The theme of the event was "Seasons of Life." As a television meteorologist, I have spent my entire career studying the changing seasons in the atmosphere. In many ways, life's journey unfolds in similar seasons.

My book, called *Brighter Skies Ahead: Forecasting A Full Life When You Empty The Nest,* tackles this painful season-changing truth for all parents: one day, the children will grow up and move away, ushering in the "Empty Nest" season.

As I met with the team at Faith Hospice, Bereavement Manager Janet Jaymin dissected an advance copy of my book and outlined the real reason why the empty nest transition is so difficult. She recognized this season-changing melancholy as a time of grief. Chapter by chapter, Janet identified for me how emptying the nest sends parents on a grief and bereavement journey.

And it doesn't stop there.

The loss of anything important can bring on feelings of grief—a relationship, a job, or even an experience. According to the Faith Hospice website, a three-year study conducted by Amerispeak and WebMD *before* COVID-19 found that 57 percent of Americans were grieving in some way at any given time: a loved one, a marriage, a career, a relationship, a beloved pet, or even human connection. That means, if you were to walk down the street or stop in a store, every other person you see would be dealing with some sort of grief. With the losses produced by the global pandemic, many experts suggest that number is now closer to 100 percent. Most of us are grieving the loss of certain experiences and "normal" life. From graduations and proms to sporting events, weddings, and even funerals, grief has become a commonplace reality.

While our initial connection was centered around the changing seasons of life and the "Empty Nest" season, *Grieving Well* is for those who are grieving the passing of a loved one. In her career, Janet Jaymin has provided essential counsel for thousands of individuals and families on the grief and bereavement journey. This book, like her entire career, is dedicated to helping those suffering pain and loss to experience a process she calls "Grieving Well."

Terri DeBoer

Introduction

Death is nothing else but going home to God, the bond of love will be unbroken for all eternity.

Mother Teresa

There is a universal truth for each of us: our time on Earth will one day come to an end. Just as we all live, each of us will die. Some of us will live for decades, finishing this life with gray hair and wrinkles. Some will live for only a few years . . . or days . . . or hours.

Death. It is a fact of life. A part of the circle of life, some say.

Yet most of us don't like to talk about it or even think about it. We put off our estate planning and the crafting of our wills because the very act of preparing for the end of life makes it seem all too real.

Even more difficult than grappling with thoughts about our mortality is the gut-wrenching pain of losing someone we love. When we lose someone special to us, we have a memorial service and a funeral. There is a time of mourning—when our grief journey begins. But it's a season of loss we must endure.

How does that season of grief unfold?

Is there such a thing as a normal period of grief?

After a loss, will there ever be fullness and happiness or even joy in life again?

If the loss is tremendously personal—a child, parent, sibling, spouse—we might wonder how we will ever go on.

In the book of Ecclesiastes in the Bible, we get a divine answer to all of those questions.

ECCLESIASTES 3:1–8, KJV

To everything there is a season, and a time to every purpose under the heaven:

A time to be born, and a time to die; a time to plant, and a time to pluck up that which is planted;

A time to kill, and a time to heal; a time to break down, and a time to build up;

A time to weep, and a time to laugh; a time to mourn, and a time to dance;

A time to cast away stones, and a time to gather stones together; a time to embrace, and a time to refrain from embracing;

A time to get, and a time to lose; a time to keep, and a time to cast away;

A time to rend, and a time to sew; a time to keep silence, and a time to speak;

A time to love, and a time to hate; a time of war, and a time of peace.

In His Word, God promises us that (aside from His love), everything else in this life is temporary. The best of times and the worst of times are temporary. As we walk through a season of grief, these promises give us hope and an assurance that this season of deep pain and loss will one day be replaced with feelings of happiness, fulfillment, and even joy.

Not only is grieving incredibly painful, but often, it is also lonely. People experiencing intense grief can almost become invisible to the world, feeling as though they are leading a hidden life within society. In some ways, it can seem as though they have inherited a deadly disease just because they are grieving. While grief is not contagious, it is universal. According to The World Counts website, sixty million people die every year worldwide,[1] which is an overwhelming number. Take a moment to let that sink in. *Sixty million people.* That is two people every second! In the United States alone, the Centers for Disease Control reports more than three million people die each year,[2] or one person every ten seconds. One more startling statistic surrounds a significant jump in deaths due to the COVID-19 pandemic. According to Shannon Sabo and Sandra Johnson, "Deaths in the United States increased by 19% between 2019 and 2020 following the onset of the COVID-19 pandemic in March 2020; the largest spike in one hundred years."[3]

This begs some questions: How are we supporting those who are left behind to endure grief? How do we even hear about or listen to those who are grieving?

In society, we talk about the concept of "dying well," allowing a patient to have a comfortable and dignified end-of-life experience.

We also need to challenge ourselves and others to think about the responsibility we have for those who are left behind—not only to *not* forget them, but also to take a step forward in helping those individuals "grieve well."

We cannot put grief into a nicely wrapped package or allow it to be pathologized, leaving survivors feeling as if they are abnormal or have been defeated because they could not save their loved ones. Let's face it; our society loves to win, and "losing to death" is hard to accept. It leaves those who are bereaved feeling they have no value, nothing left to give or live for. These feelings of worthlessness are even more reasons to offer support in helping people grieve well.

Individuals who grieve well are those who have the opportunity to tell their stories repeatedly, especially as they are reemerging from the destruction of death. Expressing the feelings of one's grief may be the number- one way to begin the healing process, but we need places to do this. *Safe places.* We must establish places that allow us to feel an array of emotions without judgment and simply allow the healing process to unfold.

Grieving Well is about the expression of our thoughts and feelings in a safe space where we are embraced for what we are experiencing. Grieving well is not about fixing because grieving well does not mean people are broken. More importantly, we must allow for opportunities for the bereaved to express themselves while we open our hearts to the humanity of grief, allowing individuals and families to climb to the highest mountain and yell at the top of their lungs that their relationship mattered.

This doesn't mean we will ever forget or stop loving the person who has passed away. Of course, that will never happen! Grieving well will help us honor and remember and celebrate our loved ones as we move into a "new season" of life, one without that special person physically here with us.

In September 2022, Faith Hospice marked a milestone in helping the bereaved navigate the painful process of "grieving well," dedicating a special space for those walking through the season of grief. This bereavement center is a physical space focused on both hope and healing for those who are still a part of this life, a space that celebrates our losses with tears, laughter, grace, love, and compassion while embracing our memories.

While there is no "typical" journey of grief, the purpose of this book is to help those who are walking through a season of grief or those who may know someone on that painful journey. Our prayer is for *Grieving Well* to serve as a sourcebook for information as well as provide insight and inspiration.

We've designed this to be an easy-to-read resource, mixing important clinical information with powerful essays written by individuals who have been on unique journeys of grief. You will read stories written by people who have lost children, parents, spouses, and siblings. Some of these deaths were sudden and unexpected; others followed long illnesses. In many cases, these individuals are keeping the memories of their loved ones alive by doing volunteer work or even creating organizations in honor of the life that ended too soon. This book will also examine God's Word on life and death, featuring thirty special devotions in Section 3, each written by pastors and spiritual leaders who counsel individuals walking through life's final hours and their loved ones.

Chapter 1
The Grief Begins

So it's true; when all is said and done,
grief is the price we pay for love.
E.A. Buccianeri

Grief is a powerful word. Just using it might bring up deep sorrow. *The American Psychological Association Dictionary of Psychology* defines grief this way: ". . . the anguish experienced after significant loss, usually the death of a beloved person. Grief is often distinguished from bereavement and mourning. Not all bereavements result in a strong grief response, and not all grief is given public expression. Grief often includes physiological distress, separation anxiety, confusion, yearning, obsessive dwelling on the past, and apprehension about the future. Intense grief can become life-threatening through disruption of the immune system, self-neglect, and suicidal thoughts. Grief may also take the form of regret for something lost, remorse for something done, or sorrow for a mishap to oneself."[4]

The death of someone we love comes immediately and co-exists with much activity and many decisions to make. The closer our relationship with the person who passed, the more significant and the higher the number of decisions to be made. From the visitation to the funeral, many logistics fall on us. There's so much to do and so many other people around that it might seem like there is no time to think—or feel. Most people compare this time to being in shock, perhaps a divine gift from our Creator that allows us to get through the minute-by-minute, hour-by-hour, and day-by-day activities that are essential in the post-death process: the visitation, the funeral, the burial, and more.

At some point, that flurry of activity ends, and we are alone.

Alone with our feelings.

Alone with our sadness.

Alone with our grief.

Hours turn into days; days turn into weeks, and weeks turn into months and eventually years. The gaping hole in our hearts and life continues to exist, and we long for healing and peace. We crave for the normalcy of our lives to be returned.

WHEN DOES "NORMAL" LIFE RETURN?

This is a difficult question to answer because the hard truth is that life will never again be the same. There will always be some part of you missing. While our society may urge you to move on, there is a much different perspective to consider, which is finding a way to move *forward*.

Our loved ones are not coming back, so what do we do? At this point, we have to find the strength within and cherish and embrace what we have not lost, which are our memories. The reality is: no one or thing can steal our memories—not even death. Grieving is such hard work and so exhausting, as human beings we are unrelenting and can find our truth within to decide how we want to live. It will not be easy, nor will it be the same for everyone, but we can create a new normalcy for the next chapter.

Unfortunately, there has not been a widely available effort to help us adjust to this grief journey, which is where the need and work of bereavement counselors, like Janet Jaymin and her team at Faith Hospice, become essential.

I (Terri) begin with asking Janet the question, "How personal is the work you do?"

From Janet

This is the most personal work I have ever done, and I cannot imagine doing anything else. I chose this profession, but more importantly, I believe it chose me. It chose me at a young age, and the path was never easy—nor was it a straight line—but the work has been as personal as I can remember.

The work is about a greater vision, a vision of helping people meet their emotional potential in a healthy way. It has always been about the people and caring for the needs of others. I have always said, *how can I have a meaningful life if my work isn't meaningful?* My work may not be profound to some, but for me, it is totally self-driven by the empathy within the depths of my being. This work goes beyond anything I can imagine, and it certainly is larger than I am.

GRIEF COUNSELING

Describe the process that takes place in counseling. Does the person who is grieving come in and have to do all of the talking, does the counselor do the talking, or is it a combination of both?

From Janet

Let me answer this question by describing my theoretical approach to counseling. As a grief counselor, I help individuals process their feelings of loss while being present with them. I validate that what *was* will never be the same, and the new journey or path will be forever—for as long as they are part of this life. These thoughts and feelings can represent a sense of doom and gloom for the individual coming to see me for grief counseling. The individual now realizes I cannot cure their grief. I help individuals by being a safe, non-judgmental person, one who sits with them to process their grief alongside them, working toward the development of positive outcomes for how they will choose to live the rest of their lives. Therefore, as a counselor, I help individuals when they're ready to receive help.

I use a client-centered approach called Humanistic Therapy, meaning I allow for free expression from the client, with no judgment from the counselor (me). As the counselor, I provide unconditional acceptance and assist with the understanding of emotions and thoughts so the individual, when ready, will begin to find hope and meaning in life. The process is one of getting to know each other using communication between the counselor and the individual seeking counseling.

I always say the initial step is the hardest, and after that, it gets easier, less intimidating, and more comfortable. I want folks to feel relaxed, to know they are in a safe space, so they can discuss the issues troubling them.

I focus on listening intently to each individual. I listen to the words spoken, which allows for the exploration of feelings or areas of concern. I observe their body language to look for non-verbal cues. I will often provide some non-threatening insight and validation filled with empathy while beginning to summarize the issues that have been brought forth. This helps the individual feel understood and, more importantly, heard. As rapport and trust develop, the relationship between the counselor and the individual becomes more comfortable. We develop a therapeutic relationship in which we both have a vested interest. The counselor's interest is in the individual being honest, forthright, and open about issues of concern, while the individual's interest is in the counselor who is assisting them as they both work toward the best possible outcomes.

GUILT AND GRIEF

When does guilt cross into the grieving process?

From Janet

I really cannot say there is a specific time in which guilt crosses into the grieving process.

What I can honestly say is that we can feel guilty at any moment while grieving because guilt is an emotion that is often part of the grieving process. Sometimes, guilt is felt as a way to avoid dealing with the pain of grief. Consider it this way; If I am dealing with the guilt, then I do not need to deal with my grief, which is incredibly more painful.

Guilt with loss is often the result of our self-reflection of the relationship we shared with the deceased. Think about it: We might feel guilt for what we did not say or what we should have said or could have said while reflecting on our relationship.

For example, when my mother died, I started to review my life by asking these questions:

"Were you a good enough daughter?"

"Did you do enough?"

"Did you say the right things?"

"Did you say the wrong things?"

I was working on my guilt from loss when I was introduced to Terri DeBoer and her book, *Brighter Skies Ahead*. I thought reading Terri's book would give me a break from dealing with guilt, but something much more transpired. I never thought that I would find what I needed where I did! Let me explain.

I had taken time out of my weekend to read *Brighter Skies Ahead,* and I came to Chapter 37, "An Empty Nest Carol." In this chapter, Terri discusses moving into adulthood and leaving her parents. She speaks of her communication with them—particularly with her mother—becoming less than it once was, but it was this next statement, her truth, that was life-changing for me:

> *I was not looking to escape my parents as much as I was branching out to make my way in the world; the distance, physical and other, was not because I was pushing away from them; I was moving toward my new way of life.*[5]

Those words gave me pause and freed me from my self-inflicted feelings of guilt as I grieved the loss of my mother. In fact, I felt I could breathe again. I had no idea I would find this in Terri's book, and she had no idea that her book had helped me with my personal guilt. Terri is just now learning, as all of you are, how her words changed my life.

The point is, I believe guilt is often about the veracity of our own truth, which takes time. It is a process. It does not happen overnight. We have to be brave, to seek out areas for personal growth and development as a way to help us navigate to those personal truths. Otherwise, guilt will eat us alive, harming us emotionally, when it is not warranted.

DIFFERENT TYPES OF LOSS

Is there a certain kind of loss that is most painful?
(The loss of a child, perhaps?)

From Janet

I believe all significant losses that we as individuals experience are painful because they are relational and deeply personal. I love the way Dr. Caroline Leaf, a communication pathologist and cognitive neuroscientist, addresses this issue. She states, "Suffering is not a competition; it is a time for compassion. We need to stop comparing who has the most pain or reason to be in pain because this takes away from actually helping each other. We also need to stop thinking we have to have a certain level of loss or traumatic event to have permission to grieve."[6]

Let's stop making grief a competitive event. Rather, let us take steps to become a strong foundation for humanity in helping each other to grieve well. We, as a society, can change this course of thinking by stopping the comparison game and creating a judgmental assessment regarding our personal loss or losses.

> *How is the grief process and counseling similar for people*
> *who are going through other types of loss/grief (e.g., divorce,*
> *the loss of another relationship, the loss of a pet, the loss of a*
> *home, the loss of a job/career, or the loss of an experience—*
> *perhaps due to COVID)?*

The style of counseling would not necessarily change due to the type of loss. Remember, a loss is anything we feel deprived of having. Loss brings about deep sadness. What had been will never be again. With any type of loss, I think it is hard for people to look at celebrating what *is* while being thankful for what *was*.

REFLECTIONS
- How long have I been on my journey of grief?
- What do I need that will help me?
- How can I lean on others to help me?

Chapter 2
Is There A "Normal" Grief Journey?

___

The only prescription for grief is having the opportunity and space to "Grieve Well."

Janet Jaymin

The folks who have been participants in my support groups [Janet speaking] over the past decade would laugh at the phrase "normal grief journey." The response I consistently get is *What is normal about a journey of intense pain that others do not understand unless they have experienced it themselves?* Think about the words in that statement. You might feel the pain produced by knowing the grief journey came too soon.

Let me rephrase "normal grief journey" this way: First, let's take out the word *normal*. Grief is individualized and unique. Next, the journey is a personal pilgrimage, often to unknown places and wrestling with new and raw emotions. Finally, our grief journey is *ours*, a personal path to walk, and no two paths are alike.

As human beings, we all like to think we can deal with the stressors of life, including the grief that comes with loss, and the thought of asking for help can make us feel defeated. So what can we do? At times, we just need to swallow our pride and take a leap of faith by reaching out to ask for a listening ear, an independent voice—someone who is a trained bereavement professional.

Remember, they are there to assist in a multitude of ways, whether it be to teach coping strategies, validate feelings, or provide a safe space to process your recent loss. Grief counselors will help with identifying goals and looking at possible solutions to any issues that cause emotional pain. They help build on your strengths while embracing positive change.

What is grief counseling? It might best be defined by Dr. Alan Wolfelt, who has stated, "The overall goal of helping grieving people is reconciliation, not resolution." Simply meaning, the goal of grief counseling is to help individuals find peace within themselves. It is not about fixing people, as people who grieve do not need to be fixed.

We must remember that people who are grieving are not part of an assembly line, and counseling is not about conforming to standard dimensions it's about an individualized process. As a bereavement counselor, I listen attentively to what a person is telling me. I listen for frustration, sadness, joy, and hope, and then I identify the need for validation and reassurance so those who come to see me know they are not alone on this path of grief. As a bereavement counselor, I help individuals see that life does change; we change, and we grow, and by understanding what intense loss is, we become better people for our experiences. The goal becomes assisting people with forward movement as they lean back into life with all its responsibilities and struggles, while understanding they still exist in the present as part of the here and now.

Over the years, I am often asked by family, friends, and acquaintances, "Why do you work in grief?" My answer comes from the quote of an unknown author: I do this "because, with each person I see, I may be the only person in their life willing to listen or feel their pain." If that does not inspire awe or reverence, I for sure, would not know what would.

REFLECTIONS
- How have I approached my grief journey?
- How may I have placed any self-imposed expectations on my grief journey?
- In what ways have I allowed myself to have a personalized journey of grief?

Chapter 3

Is There A Timeline For Grief?

*Because we have a cultural belief system that says grief should
be over once you've passed that first year mark, most people
think you should be back to normal once that "Year of Firsts"
is done. Nothing could be further from the truth.*

Megan Devine, *Refuge in Grief*

The thought of a timetable for grief is absurd. There is no timetable for grief. For example, you don't grieve for twelve months, then it is gone, and you do not have to worry about it again. Wow, that would be marvelous! You only must grieve for twelve months following the death of someone you were married to for fifty-plus years. *Not!* The thing is, we never get over the loss of someone we love, and why would we even want to? We forever love and care about those who have held significant space in our lives. At some point in time, our open wounds begin to crust over with healing, and eventually, there is a scar—a forever reminder of our loss. One's grief does not go away; it just gets fainter or softer, and honestly, that is the best way I can describe it.

TED Talks feature brief, educational, and inspirational presentations by experts and everyday people who address all topics and issues. A search on their website for the topic of grief brings a couple of personal perspectives to the question about a so-called timeline. Two powerful presentations were made by young women who had lost their husbands. Their stories are honest and real and include the loving memories of the men they lost. They also provide hope for the future.

In her talk from May 5, 2017, titled "When Someone You Love Dies, There is No Such Thing as Moving On"[7], Kelley Lynn opens her soul in a poignant and inspirational message that lasts less than seventeen minutes. Her video has already received more than two million views.

The other inspirational talk comes from Nora McInerny, who lost a pregnancy, her father, and her husband within a few short months. In her talk, dated April 25, 2019 and titled "We Don't Move On from Grief. We Move Forward with It,"[8] McInerny shares her story of loss and heartache in fifteen minutes, along with her strategies for embracing and understanding grief. Nearly one million people have watched this powerful message, in which she beautifully describes her realization that grief is chronic and a grieving person will never be "fixed;" a grieving person will laugh again and love again . . . but that person will not "move on."

REFLECTIONS

- Do you have expectations of a timeline for your grief? Do others have them for you?
- How are you comforted by knowing the grief journey does not have a timeline?
- How does it help to hear the moving stories from others who are on similar journeys?

Chapter 4

What Are The Stages Of Grief?

—

The reality is that you will grieve forever. You will not "get over" the loss of a loved one; you'll learn to live with it. You will heal and you will rebuild yourself around the loss you have suffered. You will be whole again, but you will never be the same. Nor should you be the same, nor would you want to.
Elisabeth Kubler-Ross and David Kessler, *On Grief and Grieving*

Elisabeth Kubler-Ross took a difficult topic and published a book in 1969 called *On Death and Dying.* Death is an unpopular topic, even today. People shy away from the words *death* and *dying.*

From Janet

I remember when I was young, my older sister did a book report on Elisabeth Kubler-Ross's book. What is so significant is that, even at the age of six, I understood the words *death* and *dying*, and my reaction was complete fear. I had already internalized the concept that death is bad. I believe fear is the driving force behind our death-phobic society today. It seems that most of our culture believes this is a truth that, if ignored, will somehow go away.

We've likely all heard of the Five Stages of Grief[9]. They are:

- Stage 1: Denial—avoidance, confusion, elation, shock, fear
- Stage 2: Anger—frustration, irritation, anxiety
- Stage 3: Bargaining—struggling to find meaning, reaching out to others, telling one's story
- Stage 4: Depression—overwhelm, helplessness, hostility, flight
- Stage 5: Acceptance—exploring options, new plan in place, moving on

Does everyone experience all of the stages?

From Janet

What is important to know about the five stages of grief is not everyone will go through all of them, and more importantly, we need to remember they are not linear. For example, many grieving people experience death as a welcome event, especially when a loved one has endured a long, painful illness. This would be **Acceptance**. There is nothing wrong with accepting a loved one's death.

It was never intended that individuals go through the stages of grief in order. The stages are emotions, and people vacillate from one stage to another. Some people may only experience one or two stages, while others may experience all of them. Still others, none. It is important to remember there is no right or wrong way to grieve, and we all grieve differently.

I would be remiss if I did not clarify that Elizabeth Kubler-Ross had introduced the stages for patients who had been diagnosed with a terminal illness when she was studying death and dying. As the stages caught on, they were taught to various groups of people, who then began to apply them to other areas of life—one being those who grieve. Remember the stages are a set of emotions and as human beings, we experience many of them; especially when grieving. Some people will quickly transition through a series of emotions, while others take longer. There is no right or wrong way. What you begin to see or witness with an individual is forward movement—what I like to call walking back into life again. It's the forward movement of healthy independence.

REFLECTIONS
- Have you examined the stages of grief recently?
- If you're grieving, which stage are you in now?
- How might you use the outline of these stages to prepare for what may come next?

Chapter 5
Taking Care Of Yourself

In the beginning, we focus on the pain. We see only the loss. We miss you and "us." It's easy to forget about me. Taking care of yourself is imperative for the grief process. Mind, body, and soul all need extra care to help with the journey ahead. It's not selfish. It's essential.

Danielle Simpson, Grow Through Grief

I (Janet) like to remind people that grief takes time, and though the passage of time will almost always help ease the constant pain, this process doesn't happen overnight. Grief is a process, and within the process, you must take care of yourself.

What is self-care? It is an act that promotes our social, spiritual, physical, emotional, and mental health. Good self-care can lead to positive outcomes. Remember, having **Balance** is key while incorporating life's activities: prayer, rest, work, and play.

Here are a few self-care strategies to consider (these are practical strategies and are not intended to be all-inclusive):

1. Keep decision-making to a minimum, and avoid making significant changes in your life for at least a year.

2. Keep expectations realistic or have none. Unrealistic expectations can be a set-up for disappointment.

3. Try to eat healthy meals, get enough rest, and drink plenty of water.

4. Exercise as appropriate or recommended by your physician.

5. Share your thoughts and feelings with a safe person—someone who is there to listen and not fix. Having a safe person to talk with about how you feel can often help ease intense feelings of loss. Let friends know that you do not expect advice; you just want to share and reminisce about your loved one.

6. Participate in social activities. Being home alone can leave you in the depths of your grief, so make a point to go out to lunch with friends or join a social group.

7. Take refuge in your religious practices. If you are a regular churchgoer, attending services may help you deal with grief. Private prayer, meditation, and listening to religious music are other ways to cope with the spiritual aspects of grieving.

8. Memorialize your loved one. If the person you are grieving had a strong connection to a specific cause or charity, you may consider volunteering or donating in that person's memory.

9. Be gentle with yourself; emotions are to be experienced fully. It's appropriate to allow yourself grace.

10. Read any book you want.

11. Listen to music.
12. Schedule a massage.
13. Add aromatherapy to your daily routine. Lavender is great for relaxation.
14. Engage in small acts of kindness; doing something for others is very therapeutic.
15. Breathe.
16. Plan a day trip with a friend.
17. Socialize with family and friends.
18. Laugh.
19. Keep a journal.
20. Nurture yourself.
21. Join a grief support group.
22. Contact a grief counselor.

For many of us, helping others is easier than helping ourselves, so we need to remember that grieving well takes courage. Stay engaged; speak the truth about who you are and want to be. We are resilient human beings and have a purpose in this life. With purpose, it may be just the right time to overtly love ourselves and take a chance by reaching out and asking for help. Do not let grief steal from your heart what was, is, or can be; embrace the gift of your life.

REFLECTIONS
- What am I doing to care for myself?
- How can I put together a strategy to ensure I will take care of myself?
- What is an area of my life that could benefit from self-care (physical, social, emotional, spiritual)?

Chapter 6
How Can We Help Others Who Are Grieving?

When someone is going through a storm, your silent presence
is worth more than a million empty words.
Thelma Davis

In my experience, it's not what people say so much as what people don't say.

When facing grief and heartbreak, words themselves don't mean as much as the love and care in which they are delivered. It doesn't matter if the message of comfort comes out in a mix of fumbling, imperfect words. What matters is that the person grieving feels seen and their suffering shared in friendship.

I remember the weeks after my dad and brother died. They were, obviously, devastating losses. The comfort and small acts of kindness from friends, neighbors, clients, and colleagues got me through those really hard times. What surprised me, though, was how my grief caused some friends to feel uncomfortable. Some of them sent flowers or a card to represent their sympathy but then never addressed me personally. They never called to ask how I was doing or share a simple "I'm here for you." Instead, they acted as though it had never happened, moving on to whatever distracting topic of conversation they could find—anything but face the reality that things were not back to normal.

There are a couple of factors that contribute to this isolation, which many grieving people experience as I did. First, seeing someone else grieve is like looking into a mirror; it reflects our own fears and mortality. We realize there is no escaping these painful seasons. Eventually, we will all be in their shoes. To make matters worse, people are afraid of offending someone or making a misstep. So, out of fear of saying the wrong thing, they say nothing at all. On top of that, the digital communication era has created a generation of people who rely on texting, emojis, and memes to express their feelings—all of it masked behind a screen—propelling the natural way of communicating from the heart into a lost art.

The next time you're wondering what to say to someone who is grieving, remember this: It does not matter that you say anything special, memorable, or perfect. It just matters that you say something.

COMFORTING PHRASES AND CONVERSATION STARTERS

- "I know there is nothing I can say to take away your pain. But I want you to know that I am here for you."
- "Would talking about [name] be okay, or would you like to talk about something else?"

- "Is there a memory that keeps coming up for you?"
- "How is [name of another family member/grieving person] coping right now?"
- "I baked my favorite muffins for you and will be leaving them on the doorstep this afternoon. I'm happy to visit, too, if you want some company today or any other time."
- "I just want to let you know I am thinking about you today. You have been on my mind lately. How are you?"
- "I know it's the first holiday without [name], and I want to let you know I'm thinking about you."

Emily Richette
(TV Host & Podcaster, The AMPLIFY Show) contributed to this section

---

REFLECTIONS
- Can you think of someone you know who has lost a loved one?
- How can you use Emily's suggestions to reach out and connect?
- If you feel uncomfortable because you don't know what to say, how can you find helpful information?

MY GRIEF JOURNEY

*We bereaved are not alone. We belong to the largest company
in the world—the company of those who have known suffering.*
Helen Keller, *We Bereaved*

In the following pages, you will read personal stories shared by those who have been on personal grief journeys.

These essays reveal the deep pain and profound heartache as each individual continues to seek out and find peace and hope after experiencing intense loss.

The first is from *Grieving Well* author Janet Jaymin, offered as a story when her co-author, Terri DeBoer, asked, "Why did you choose grief/bereavement for your career?"

May all of our grief sojourners' words provide you with inspiration and encouragement.

My Grief Journey: Janet Jaymin

> **Why did you choose grief/bereavement for your career?**

When I was a young child, I learned I had a cousin who had died at the age of eighteen. It was *how* she died that stuck with me. My cousin, Dee, was preparing for high school graduation. She had been a cheerleader in high school and was beautiful, popular, and extremely bright. My mother told me she had the whole world in front of her. Dee's parents, my aunt and uncle, owned several restaurants, and Dee was needed, and expected, to help with the family business, and she did.

The story goes that my Aunt Helen, Dee's mother, asked her to run home to retrieve the homemade pies for the restaurant. My aunt and uncle were busy working, and after a couple of hours, they started to wonder what had happened to Dee and the pies. Finally, my aunt decided to run home to check on Dee. When my aunt arrived home, she experienced a mother's nightmare; her only daughter was lying on the floor in a pool of blood, dead, from a self-inflicted gunshot wound. My eighteen-year-old cousin, who seemed to have the brightest future, had killed herself. My mother said the family was shocked, and suicide in the 1950s, according to my mother, was nearly unheard of. My mother shared how people had been so judgmental toward the family members—as if they had pulled the trigger and killed her themselves. She told me how hurtful it was, and when she spoke, she choked up with tears in her eyes. As an eight-year-old, I was baffled that people could be so cruel.

I had never met my cousin since I had not yet been born when she died. I learned about my cousin through the stories my mother shared. I was intrigued with my cousin's story, especially when my mother would get to the part of her being pregnant with me at the time. Mother told me that her doctor had said to expect a December baby. My mother would smile while telling me this story because her sister Helen (Dee's mother) would tell my mother, "Have the baby on Dee's birthday," which would have made me a November baby.

Well, I was born on Dee's Birthday. I was well aware that this was an incredible honor. In fact, I became somewhat special to Dee's parents, my aunt and uncle; though, I always felt my birthday was over-shadowed by the loss of Dee. I became a reminder of her death. Because of this, I experienced my birthday as something lonely and sad, not special.

It just was. My birthday was a reminder of the grief experienced by my family, and really, how could that reminder ever be changed or fixed? At times as a youngster, I wondered if I would continue the pattern of suicide in our family. As a kid, this became a hauntingly and frightening experience.

I spent many nights awake, looking to the sky with amazement, taking solace in the beautiful stars and constellations. It was the night sky that brought peace to my thoughts, and it helped me overcome my fear of thinking I would die by suicide. I must point out that I never had a plan to hurt myself, and I never shared any of these intense feelings with a single soul. I did not want any attention drawn to myself; it was enough that others and I were reminded of Dee's death every November. For years, I had begged God to bring Dee back, but of course, it never happened.

I lived with the shame that comes with suicide. I knew the shame was not warranted, but I still felt it. It was the shame you feel inside, the unseen shame. I certainly never wanted anyone to know this dreadful story, as I figured I would be risking hurtful judgment from society, but to my amazement, it was this exact story, along with the incredible amount of grief that I witnessed from my family, that attracted me to the field of counseling. I knew I wanted to work with people hurting from loss, and I wanted to do it with kindness; no judgment and without shaming. Ever since I can remember, I have gravitated to those who are hurting from the death and dying experience.

Over the years, I have been reminded of the emotional pain I experienced as a child, feeling so alone and helpless about the death of my cousin, along with witnessing the grief my family experienced. As a youngster, I was well aware of the intense sense of self I had and did not want others to hurt emotionally.

I have experienced the death of my grandparents, parents, beloved brother-in-law, aunts, uncles, cousins, and friends. Do I ever get sad? Do I ever miss them, and do I ever want to hug them or talk with them again? Absolutely—in fact, all of the time—but I remind myself that I am incredibly blessed to have known and loved each of these individuals in my life.

I'm grateful to have been born to a loving family. The family who helped shape the person I am today. *Wow, I have so many gifts.* I tell myself over and over that it is these gifts, shared by those who have gone before us, that we must remember.

I used to feel my birthday was a burden—not only for me but, more importantly, for my family. Today, however, I know my date of birth was part of God's greater plan. It may have felt, when a child, that I was born only to remind my family of Dee and what she had meant to them, but I have come to peace with it and realize it was for so much more.

My Grief Journey: Jill Plasman

Gone in a Heartbeat

Our family recently celebrated the thirty-fifth anniversary of my brother's tragic passing. You would think that after three and a half decades, the details of that day would begin to diminish; ironically, as the shock wears off, the details become clearer through the years. However, let me be candid. It's amazing how the Lord allows that time to lapse, for our minds and hearts to embrace and process loss.

The year was 1986. I was a sophomore in high school, blessed with good friends and stable home life. I was a high school cheerleader, enjoying life to its fullest when it took a sudden turn. This Saturday night started like any other, a normal evening spent hanging out with friends. I came home, caught up with my parents for a few minutes, and then went to bed. My room was on the lower level of our home, and I can still hear the sound of footsteps and dogs barking before the knock on the door at approximately 6:00 a.m. Sunday morning.

As I walked up the stairs, I saw my mom grabbing a robe and heading toward the front door. When she opened the door, there a police officer stood, with his hat in his hand. He asked if this was the residence of Geffrey Reinke, to which my mom responded *yes*. By this point, my father had met her at the door, and I stood in the backdrop. The officer proceeded to share with deep sympathy that my brother had been involved in a serious accident and had passed away at the scene. I don't recall a lot after hearing those words except that the next few days were filled with endless visitors, lots of tissues, piles of sympathy cards, and countless casseroles and baked goods.

I vaguely remember the funeral—so many people—but what I remember most is that we (the immediate family) appeared to be consoling those who had shown up to pay their respects. Some people were sobbing uncontrollably; others just stared at us without words. The whole week following the accident felt surreal, almost as if we were living a nightmare from which we could not shake ourselves awake. My brother was five years older than me; he was attending college to be a dentist, and many of the faces I met during the days and weeks post-accident were new faces, sharing lots of memories and fun stories we had never heard.

One thing was clear: *he was loved.*

Enter life PGA (post-Geff's accident). Time stood still for months, maybe even years. Him being my only sibling, life was immediately and dramatically different without his presence. My parents were grieving so intensely, it felt as if I had lost them too. I moved out to attend college locally but found myself wanting to be home more than anything—close to my parents. My faith was strong but challenged. I had so many questions, and most of them began with the word "Why?"

I think one set of questions that haunted me, given my spiritual immaturity at the time, was—because my brother was so young, and we had not lost a lot of relatives before him—"What was heaven like for him? Was he alone?" Well, I can share that a couple of years PGA, I was blessed with a special dream. In this dream, my brother appeared to me. He didn't have wings or a halo, but he was dressed in white. He had several young people around him, and he spoke to me in the dream, saying, "I'm not alone. I want you to meet some of my new friends." Then, he went around the room and named them one by one—all faces and names I had never heard. I didn't want this dream to end. When I awoke, I felt different. I believed the Lord had truly blessed me with this dream, which provided me with peace beyond comprehension. The dream didn't take away the pain or the memories, but it did provide me with new feelings of comfort and hope.

You've heard it said, "Life must go on," and it did. I met the love of my life in college, someone I believe was divinely planted in my life. He's no angel, but he's definitely Heaven-sent. We often joke that my brother sent him. We had our first child in 1996, who we decided to name after my brother. A bonus is that he physically resembles my brother in so many ways. A few years later, we had a second son.

I share our new family tree because that's where it still really hurts. Last night, my youngest son said to me, "Mom, do you ever stop and wonder how different our lives would be if Uncle Geff was alive?" It's so crazy that my boys, now twenty-five and twenty-one have never met their uncle, who was such a huge part of my life. He has physically missed their birthdays, holidays, special school and sporting events, and more. To help with this, we keep his memory alive by talking openly about the accident. We celebrate his birthday and even the date of his accident; they've seen pictures and heard many stories. I tell them all of the time how lucky they are to have their own angel. I should also share that although this may be controversial to some, I was approached by a medium (who worked with local law enforcement) several years ago while I was struggling with my brother's accident. The medium delivered a brief, albeit life-changing, message to me. First, she politely asked if she could share the message with me.

I was a little freaked out but nodded. She proceeded to rattle off concise responses to the many questions that had been swirling around in my head for many years.

Again, I respect everyone's opinion, and you are entitled to your own; but for me, this was a moment that paved the way for so much healing. I believe the Lord answered my prayers in such a direct yet unique way. From that point forward, I knew the signs I received were from my brother, letting me know that he is with me. I know when his song (from his funeral) comes on the radio at the exact time I need to hear it, it comes from my brother, and I know that I will see my brother again in Heaven. *That's* what keeps me going.

I don't want to paint a picture that this tragedy is all rainbows and gumdrops. There are many times (even today) that losing him just plain sucks. However, when I find myself going down the "this sucks" road, I force myself to stop and regroup. I try to work my grief for good and be there for others. After all, that is what He and my brother would want.

> ### In closing, I recently read the following from an unknown author. It spoke volumes:

I had my notion of grief.

I thought it was the sad time that followed the death of someone you love.

And you had to push through it to get to the other side.

But I'm learning there is no other side.

There is no pushing through.

But rather, there is absorption. Adjustment. Acceptance.

And grief is not something you complete, but rather, you endure.

Grief is not a task to finish and move on,
But an element of yourself—
An alteration of your being.
A new way of seeing.
A new definition of self.

My Grief Journey: Gerilyn May

The Loss of My Precious Son

When others ask me how many children I have, I make some people uncomfortable when I respond, "I have two sons. One is an ER doctor in Minnesota, and one is in Heaven." It took me months to say the words aloud: "Stephen died." I just couldn't force those words to come out of my mouth.

On April 28, 2010, an unspeakable event happened to our family. Our incredible, loving son, Stephen, at age seventeen, passed away from a tragic accident in our home. I had gone for a walk and came home to find him unresponsive in our basement. In the chaotic moments that followed, my mind and body went numb. I was swept away from the scene to our main floor. The first paramedic to arrive was Firefighter Steve, who had cut our lawn for years and knew our family well. This was deeply personal for him, and as I kept screaming, asking him to please keep Stephen alive, he replied, "We've got this Gerilyn. We are doing everything we can." Suddenly, I was surrounded by neighbors and my sister and brother-in-law, whose friend called them after coincidentally (really a *God*-thing) they had driven by our house and seen the firetrucks. We were all praying. I was pacing around like a zombie and crying out loud to the Lord to save my son. "*Please* don't take him from us!"

I had to call my husband, Jamie, at work, and the words wouldn't come out of my mouth, so he dropped everything and drove straight home. I don't remember much more of those moments—except a firefighter, who I'd grown up with, saying to me, "I'm sorry . . . your son has died."

NO, NO, NO!!!! This can't be happening! I collapsed in disbelief. Our other son, Brett, arrived home after being picked up at Hope College, and together, we tried to process what had just occurred. Our family of four was suddenly a family of three. My heart felt as though it had just been ripped viciously from my chest.

My sister and brother-in-law, Mary and Bob, had the task of talking with our local Gift of Life representative because Stephen had "checked that box" on his driver's license that made him an organ donor. By then, hundreds of Stephen's friends and their families began arriving at our home and were wandering around in our yard, hugging each other and sobbing. I'm sure the universe could hear their cries of sorrow.

Weeks after his death, it was determined that Stephen had been attempting a strengthening technique that he had watched in a video, and it had gone very wrong. Had someone been with him, this tragedy wouldn't have happened, but he had chosen to try this technique alone. We are grateful to the Kent County Sheriff and Silent Observer, who fielded phone calls from teenagers who suspected they knew what Stephen had tried.

Grief is excruciatingly painful—physically, emotionally, and spiritually. Like a strong Band-Aid, it rips away everything that should be in balance to survive. Healing is hard work. It's a marathon, not a sprint. Winnie, my incredible Christian grief counselor, shared that when someone experiences trauma as I did, it "fries" every fiber of their being. It's like sticking your finger in a light socket, with a jolt that shocks the equilibrium out of you. The grief journey works to repair the millions of fibers that need to be healed. I tried to make excuses to miss my grief counseling sessions. Winnie, who had also lost a son and shared that she couldn't "fix" me, promised to walk beside me . . . and did for four years until I was ready to release the apron strings I was using to fiercely hold onto her.

We are blessed that family, friends, and co-workers (thank you to my incredible co-workers at Van Andel Institute) cared about and supported us unconditionally. They prayed for us when we didn't have the strength to pray for ourselves. I learned that, sometimes, we must accept vulnerability and weakness because nothing will knock you to your knees like losing a child, especially in a traumatic way.

I remember thinking crazy thoughts. Stephen and I were the Christmas-decorating team in our house; it was "our thing." When our first Christmas without him came, I wanted nothing to do with decorating, and I certainly didn't have the energy to even consider it. Our small tree, a gift from Tracy and Shannon, was later planted in our yard in memory of Stephen. I fought with myself in my mind: Do I make myself put out lights? If I do, I know they will be white to shine the light of Christ. I wanted Stephen to look down from Heaven and see that we still believed. But it never happened that first year—or the second, third, or fourth, for that matter.

I remember wanting to give up on prayer. One of our church's beloved Catholic nuns shared something I will never forget. She said, "You will always be connected to Stephen because of the love of a mother for her son. Think of your love as a brilliant strand that connects your hearts and souls. Praying will only strengthen that strand . . . and your bond." So I began fervently praying. When I experienced severe PTSD symptoms in the middle of the night, I turned to prayer. If praying strengthened my connection to my son, I would do it religiously. As I focused on prayer, my faith grew. Though I thought I was faithful before Stephen died, the depth of faith that comes from deepening your personal relationship with Jesus is immeasurable.

I always chose to put one foot in front of the other, only with the grace of God, but choosing joy came much later. Jamie and I now volunteer for Gift of Life Michigan and The Transplant Foundation since Stephen was an organ donor. His decision in life left his heart valves to save eight babies' lives; his beautiful blue eyes gave someone sight, and his strong bones and tissue were gifted to help burn victims or perhaps wounded veterans. I've spoken at events, medical transplant conferences, and the Transplant Games of America alongside three other beautiful mothers—Kathy, Sally, and Laurie, who also lost their precious children. We choose to find joy together through volunteerism and honoring our kids. We belong to the "club" that no one wants to be in. We have a silent and strong bond that will remain between us for the rest of our lives.

After Stephen died, we learned he frequently said, "ELE!"—*or everybody love everybody*! It originated from a Will Farrell movie. Will's character captained an inept basketball team and tried to keep them from fighting with opposing teams during games by yelling, "ELE!" This phrase stuck as Stephen's legacy. Many shared that he truly lived the ELE! philosophy, and his friends created shirts, designed by Stephen's Uncle Bob to remember him. They and their families raised money to endow scholarships in his name. Our dearest friend and attorney, Steve, and his wife, Renae (who met Stephen at his birth, even before I did, because of birthing complications), established a 501c3 nonprofit to bless people with inspiration to live the ELE! philosophy of understanding, compassion, and love. Unsurmountable love has been showered on us all, and it emerged from this tragedy. Helping others through ELE! brings us joy.

I'll admit that I didn't grieve well, but I learned that it's okay to not be okay. I now deeply value accepting and receiving support from a professional, from loving family, and from friends. Though we each must walk our own grief journeys, we can't (and shouldn't) do it alone. Today, Jamie and I desire to represent *hope* and *courage* to those who are grieving.

We often share that the most important things to help those that are grieving are:

1. Be PRESENT
2. Be NON-JUDGMENTAL
3. Provide UNCONDITIONAL LOVE

No one knows how they will react to acute trauma and grief. Seek faith, family, and friends. Know that you don't, and shouldn't have to, walk your grief journey alone. Loving support is available and the comfort that only our Lord can provide will always be there.

My Grief Journey: Carl Paganelli

My Journey to the Other Side of Grief

My journey began in March of 2012. It was two weeks before my youngest daughter's high school senior trip to Jamaica. My wife Cathy had a long history of cancer in her family—her dad, mother, and a younger brother had all died from cancer. Her mother died under the care of Faith Hospice at Trillium Woods.

For this reason, Cathy underwent an annual colonoscopy and endoscopy for preventive purposes. In the past, everything had been normal, but this time, the doctor appeared nervous after the procedures, and I knew something was wrong.

Cathy was diagnosed with stage 4 duodenal cancer. Cathy wouldn't cancel our daughter's senior trip, wanting our daughter to enjoy it. During the trip, we made numerous calls to doctors in the Midwest and eventually chose a local surgeon in Grand Rapids, Michigan. Cathy underwent a procedure called the "The Whipple."

After surgery, Cathy's recovery was long, and she struggled physically. After three months in the hospital, Cathy was finally released and able to start chemotherapy. Cathy's cancer was very aggressive, and doctors gave her less than a 5 percent chance of surviving five years. Over the next four and a half years, Cathy had her ups and downs, but on occasion, she was able to take trips with me while I worked as a referee in some NFL games. Cathy loved watching football.

In June of 2016, while getting treatment in Florida, we were asked for the first time, "Where would you like hospice? In Michigan or Florida?" Cathy and I knew the battle was over, and it was time to return home to Grand Rapids to prepare for her death.

Upon our arrival, Cathy was immediately hospitalized. Shortly thereafter, we met with various hospice agencies. When we met the Faith Hospice social worker, she opened with a prayer. Right then, Cathy and I knew Faith Hospice was who we wanted to care for her and prepare our family for her death.

Cathy returned home from the hospital, and the hospice process began. The Faith Hospice staff was so caring, insightful, and compassionate; everyone answered our questions completely. Faith Hospice became part of our family during the fourteen-day journey we faced just before Cathy's death.

The day Cathy died—July 14, 2016—Bereavement Counselor Janet Jaymin met with our family at our home and introduced herself to Cathy, who was, at that point, mostly unconscious. Janet very kindly assured Cathy that she would be there for her family and provide support after her death.

Janet asked me how Cathy and I met. I told her we met when she was fifteen, and then I turned to Cathy and said, "Wasn't that right Cathy?" Cathy raised her head off of the pillow and gave me one final kiss. It was a beautiful moment.

Faith Hospice and Janet were there for my family after Cathy's death, and my youngest daughter, Crysta, immediately sought counseling. My oldest daughter, Carley, lived in Florida and connected with a hospice agency there that Janet referred her to.

For me, I returned to football and tried to handle my grief by immersing myself in officiating.

In November 2016, Crysta and I met with Janet to discuss the upcoming holidays. Janet suggested we do something different for the first holiday season without Cathy. Crysta confided to Janet that I wanted to take the family on a Caribbean cruise over Christmas. Janet immediately said, "That is an awesome idea."

I spent the winter after Cathy's passing in Florida and tried to work through my grief by walking and working out. During my walks, I thought about the good times with Cathy, the suffering she went through, and our four-and-a-half-year battle with cancer. I also thought about how to move forward in life without Cathy. I thought I had everything under control.

I returned to Michigan in April 2017 and set up an appointment with Janet. I was looking for advice on how to help my daughters, both of whom were struggling with Cathy's passing, their futures, and how to move forward.

Halfway through the session, Janet asked, "How are you doing?" I hesitated, thinking about my answer, and said, "I really don't know." By the end of the session, I was in tears.

"Janet, you probably didn't think Mr. Tough Guy would need help."

She said, "You all do sooner or later."

During one of our sessions, Janet and I talked about my officiating career in the NFL. "The pressure and the stress to officiate a Super Bowl must be unbelievable," she said.

"Yes, there is . . . knowing that millions of people are watching you, and one mistake could cost a team the Super Bowl," I told her. Though, nothing compared to the pressure, stress, and anxiety I'd been dealing with trying to keep my family together and continue my life without Cathy.

For ten months, I didn't grieve, and I asked Janet when I was going to break down. She said, "You were probably grieving for the four-and-a-half years while battling cancer with Cathy."

In early June of 2017, Carley, now engaged, returned to Michigan to look at wedding venues. The night before she arrived, it finally hit me. Cathy was gone and wouldn't be with us as we made wedding decisions.

Cathy had always been the rock of the family, and I knew I had to step up and take over. I was confused, but then relented, allowing my emotions to take over . . . and I finally started grieving. I called Janet to help me work through the pain. She explained that the sense of losing Cathy and her not being with us to make those decisions triggered my grief.

June was not a good month trying to pick a wedding venue and preparing for the first-year anniversary of Cathy's passing.

In addition, I had to prepare for the annual NFL officiating clinic. For weeks before the clinic, I saw Janet and talked about skipping the clinic. Janet coached me, saying, "Cathy would want you to attend the clinic with no expectations."

The first day of the clinic was the first-year anniversary of Cathy's death. It was harder than expected, and I firmly realized Cathy wasn't coming back. On the last night of the clinic, I asked God to take the grief and pain from me. I woke up the next morning with a sense that a burden had been lifted from my shoulders. It was my time to live life, choose happiness, and create new memories because that's what Cathy would want for me.

Without the support of Faith Hospice and Janet, my daughters and I would still be struggling. A Bible verse that perfectly sums up the way Cathy lived her life is 2 Timothy 4:7: "I have fought the good fight, I have finished the race, I have kept the faith." No matter what Cathy was dealing with, no matter how tough life got, she never stopped keeping the faith. She was a true inspiration to our family and the many lives she touched.

My Grief Journey: Dianne Reed

Alone for the First Time

When I came home from my husband's funeral, my first thought was *I've never lived alone before,* and I felt frightened, just wanting the nightmare to be over and for my husband to come back home to me!

Scott and I were married almost forty years, had two grown daughters, two grandsons, and lived in the country in a cabin we had built just outside of Hastings, Michigan. We were excited about planning for retirement. We even thought about getting a small motor home and touring the United States. We had so many dreams about what we wanted to do in the future.

Then, Scott got a call from Mayo Clinic, one that contained that dreaded "*C* word," regarding results from a biopsy they had done two weeks before. The first thing I said to him was, "We're going to beat this. You'll see, and everything will be alright." We returned to Mayo Clinic to see what was needed to save Scott's life.

About six months before this, Scott had started having pain in his left shoulder and couldn't make the fingers on his left hand move at times. The neurologists at Mayo Clinic discovered cancer, synovial sarcoma, was growing inside some of the nerves under his shoulder and explained to us this was an incredibly aggressive form of cancer. They decided the only chance for him to survive was to amputate his shoulder and arm, and hopefully, that would remove all of the cancer.

A couple of months after his surgery came excruciating phantom pain, which was so heartbreaking to witness. I can't tell you how many times I called for an ambulance to take Scott to the hospital because it felt like his arm, which wasn't there anymore, was on fire. The hospital staff would always give him morphine and send him home. I asked several doctors to come up with a plan so this wouldn't keep happening, and they would simply tell me to keep bringing him back to the hospital when it happened again.

I was exasperated, and Scott was ready to end it all, when finally, a doctor suggested we contact a palliative care doctor with

Faith Hospice. This doctor had a plan and with the right combinations of medications, he was able to take Scott's pain level from a ten down to a two. Scott was able to enjoy life again with little pain and no more emergency runs to the hospital.

Unfortunately, however, his cancer spread, and three years after that scary call from Mayo Clinic, Scott died peacefully in the care of Faith Hospice Trillium Woods with our daughters and me at his side.

During those last three years of his life, we read the Bible together, prayed out loud, and listened to a chapter each night from the audiobook version of *Heaven* by Randy Alcorn. Reading and praying were practices we had previously done quietly to ourselves, but looking back, those days hold such special memories for me. Our pastor and teams from the church came out to pray with us, and I followed exactly what I read in the Bible to do to heal Scott, but that was not God's plan. Toward the end, Scott said he felt he was going fast, and he told me how much he loved me. I cried with my head on his lap and told him I was going to die of a broken heart.

How am I going to go on without him? I thought.

Grieving is not something we are taught, and I didn't know who to talk to or if it was something you just have to get through on your own. I was also trying to figure out what purpose or plan God had for me for the future. I had so many questions, most beginning with *why*.

Family and friends were always there for me, but I felt I needed to talk to others who had lost loved ones to find out how they coped. I read several books by widows and joined a Bible study. One day, I received a letter from Faith Hospice offering grief counseling, and then, another day, a letter came from Widowed Persons Group in Grand Rapids—both inviting me to join their meetings. I did take advantage of these invitations and found comfort in talking about my feelings and fears. I received guidance from group leaders and listened to others speak of how they managed along these new and unfamiliar paths.

I kept myself busy by sorting things because I knew I was going to sell our house and move closer to my daughters in the Grand Rapids area. I prayed about when to sell our home, his truck, the lawnmowers, and farm equipment; and when to tackle cleaning out the basement, shed, and pole barns. Going through his clothes was difficult; my heart broke with each new item I pulled out, but I did laugh to myself when it came to all the long-sleeved shirts and jackets I found. I had carefully cut the left sleeve off and sewn that area closed for him to wear more comfortably. After thinking about it, I decided donating those "customized shirts" would not be a good idea!

Listening to the Holy Spirit speak to me was something I never really paid much attention to before Scott's death, but so many times, things would happen that opened doors for me, allowing me to make decisions and showing me the right path to follow. I realized these thoughts and ideas that kept coming to me over and over again were from the Holy Spirit, speaking and trying to get my attention.

I also started getting what I call "God winks." The day I listed my home with a realtor, I was driving home from town and praying. *God, did I make the right decision about selling and moving?* Then, I saw a bright rainbow—one end touching down on a field of oats. The ground and oats were glowing, and I said, "Okay, Lord, thank you!" My house sold within days, and the new owners gave me the time I needed to remove all of Scott's accumulated farm equipment.

My next "God wink" came after I considered volunteering at Trillium Woods a few years later but was a little timid about returning to the place where Scott had spent his last days. I asked a friend, who worked at Holland Home, to accompany me. We walked to Scott's old room where a volunteer stood in the doorway, asking the patient if he would like him and his cat to visit. The patient replied, "Not today," so then the volunteer turned our way. I noticed he was wearing an MSU (Michigan State University) shirt, the school my husband had loved to show off too. *What a coincidence.*

I introduced myself and my friend and told the volunteer why we were there. He introduced himself and said his name was Scott! I thought it was all getting a little crazy! As volunteer Scott started to put his cat back in its cage, I asked if I could pet it. He showed me his cat and said his cat was "very special" because its left shoulder and leg had been amputated. My friend and I were astounded! It felt like God and my Scott were there with me—and would be with me every day, assuring things would be okay.

On my drive home that day, a silver Mustang, identical to the one my husband owned, passed me. It was as if Scott was saying goodbye.

I still ask the Holy Spirit to help me and guide me, and I'm still getting "God winks." Just the other night, seven years after Scott died, I dreamed that I got out of a car and there was Scott, looking so young and handsome. We embraced for a long time, and I said, "It's been so long!" I remember the background around us was glowing, and it felt so comforting and beautiful. When I woke up, I thanked God for that glimpse into Heaven and the chance to see Scott, happy and smiling at me.

Faith is how I got through all those difficult times, and faith will continue to get me through tomorrow—along with my incredible family and close friends. Sometimes, I sit quietly, close my eyes, and picture that dream of Scott greeting me in Heaven and giving me that great big hug!

My Grief Journey: Jolynn Van Wienen

My grief story began five years before our son, Seth, died. In 2002, God called my husband and me to adopt two little boys from Russia. We brought Seth and Luke home and thought our family was complete with five kids. Two years later, we found ourselves back in Russia, in the same town, at the same orphanage, meeting our next son, Andrew.

By November 2007, we had six kids, and I was six months pregnant. We were in the middle of adopting our last child (this time for Guatemala). Yeah . . . eight kids . . . crazy—yet *called*. We were so excited about the upcoming year and all that it would bring—that is until November 4. Greg and I were away for the weekend; three of the kids were with Greg's parents, and three of the boys were staying home with our amazing babysitter who treated our kids like her younger siblings.

We received a phone call saying that Seth had been hit by a car in a parking lot and was headed to the hospital. Initially, we thought, *It's probably just a broken arm or leg since it happened in a parking lot.* Our sitter, Keri, had asked if she could take the boys to her brother's state championship soccer game. We thought the boys would love it. "Of course, they can go!" we told her.

After the game was finished, Keri guided our sons—Caleb, age thirteen, Seth, age ten, and Andrew, age eight—across a divided road back to her car. Caleb and Seth ran across the first road and

Keri called ahead, asking them to wait in the median for her and Andrew. Caleb stopped. Seth didn't.

Seth was hit by a car and landed in a nearby parking lot—hence the "hit by a car in a parking lot" explanation. I know in my mom's heart that Seth died immediately. His body just didn't stop working until the next day. Leaving that hospital the following day, without our son . . . well, a part of me remained in that hospital room.

We went back to Greg's parents' house to let our other kids know what happened. We were in complete shock those first few weeks. I had to keep counting our kids to figure out why I was only counting five and not six. Often, I found myself wailing in my closet, screaming to God. "I just want him back! I just want him back!" I didn't think anything could cause me more pain—until I watched our other children. That first week, we all slept in sleeping bags on our family room floor. No one wanted to be alone, especially at night when things tend to quiet down but your mind can't. While I listened to our children cry themselves to sleep each night, I yelled at Satan. "Come after me! Hurt me, but don't you *dare* hurt our other kids!" He didn't listen.

The first day they went back to school (they were in late elementary and early middle school at the time), I got them ready for the day, prayed over them, made their lunches, and got them on the bus. Then, I went back into an empty house and found one lunch still on the counter. I had reflexively made a lunch for Seth, but of course, he wasn't there. My six-month pregnant body collapsed on the kitchen floor, wailing once again. Crying out to God, I pleaded, "Please don't make me pack just five lunches!!" I was there for over two hours begging God to take away the pain.

That's when the phone rang. Another Jenison Christian mom called and apologized over and over for bothering me. She explained that God had laid it on her heart so heavily that she just couldn't deny the command to call me. She said, "I have no idea *why*, but God wants me to pack your kids' lunches for the next two months."

That's how real God made Himself known to us in our early stages of grief. I remember telling Greg it was almost too holy of an experience.

Three months to the day after Seth's death, on February 4, 2008, I gave birth to our youngest son, Benjamin Seth. Six months later, we were in Guatemala to pick up our daughter, Lydia. Needless to say, those nine months were the biggest emotional roller coaster ever. By September, Greg and I were exhausted and needed a day to ourselves. So we found a day-long grief camp for kids in Grand Rapids, and you better believe we forced them to go. We took a respite, and at the end of it, went to pick up our kids.

One daughter, who historically does not show much emotion, was crying uncontrollably. After finally calming her down, she explained. "Mom!! I'm not the only one having nightmares!" It blew us away how quickly all of our kids were able to connect with other kids, though they had been strangers that morning! For the next three weeks, Greg and I searched for a place that was more long-term, rather than just a day-long camp, for our kids to find support. A Christ-centered place. A place where our kids could go and safely process their feelings. A place that showed them that God is still good.

There was no place.

God whispered to my heart, "I want *you* to make that place!" Boy, did I argue with Him for those three weeks. Finally, I told God that I was going to talk with Greg (a wonderful, logical, man) and tell him what I was thinking. Certainly, he would tell me that I wasn't hearing God correctly, and that would be the end of it.

Funny how we still think we have any control over our lives! I told Greg what I was hearing, and after I did, he fell to the chair sobbing—*not* the reaction I anticipated!

"Honey, you don't understand!! I've felt God telling me the exact thing, but I couldn't ask you to do that!" We had an infant who wasn't sleeping through the night, a toddler who still didn't speak any English, and He wanted us to start up a ministry. We ended up saying yes!

After a year of researching and planning how to create this place, in January 2010, Starlight Ministries held our first grief support group with twelve kids (five of which had the Van Wienen last name!) It was our three- to five-year plan to incorporate adult programming, but once again, God had different plans. Six months later, we were having adult meetings as well.

Today, Starlight holds four nights of programming in two different locations. The kids are grouped by age and adults are grouped by type of loss. We hold a three-day grief camp for kids ages seven to seventeen every summer, a four-week grief education series, a bereaved mom's retreat, a bereaved parent's night, and we just started selling a two-year Christ-centered grief curriculum. In the fall of 2020, we opened our center in Hudsonville, Michigan. It is our mission to provide safe, Christ-centered grief support to families in our communities.

My passion is to show people that even through death, *God is still good.* There is hope and healing to be had when you come together and support one another. It has been extremely healing to Greg and me to have been called to this ministry.

Some days, I still find myself crying out to God, "I just want him back!" and then He gently reminds me that He loves Seth even more than we do, and one day, while he won't come back to me, I will be able to join him! I'll be able to see his sweet little button nose, blond hair, and blue eyes. Hear his darling lisp, saying, "I love you too, Mum." Feel his little boy arms around me and smell the dirt on his hands. Oh, what a day that will be. Praise God from whom all blessings flow.

My Grief Journey: Sandi Veenkamp

Where Do I Begin?

The year 2016 began somewhat uneventfully. My husband, Nick, and I celebrated forty-eight years together. We were blessed with three wonderful children, and we were enjoying them and our grandchildren while focusing on providing care to my aging mother.

That soon changed when we found out that Nick had stage 4 prostate cancer that came with a two-year maximum life expectancy. We were in shock. The doctor talked but neither of us could comprehend the words being delivered. Suddenly, I was faced with hard facts. And questions. "What are my responsibilities for supporting Nick physically and emotionally, which he so direly needs during his cancer journey? How am I going to balance his care while offering the same to my mother who was in a hospital bed three miles away, living alone in her home and needing full-time care?" I simply did not have the time or want to face what was going on with me.

I completely shut down emotionally. I had work to do. I had four women from my church, including Kathy, the lead person caring for my mom. What a God-send! While Nick was battling cancer, I still took a shift at mom's six to seven days a week. That's when Faith Hospice came into the story. They started at mom's and transitioned into helping Nick and me. We had an amazing support system.

Never would I imagine that Nick would be the first of seven family members who would "go home" within eleven months. Nick was a hard worker and loved his family very much. As many married couples do, we had bad times and good times. Sometimes, I think remembering the "not-so-good" times got me through his passing. That way, I didn't feel guilty when I found glimmers of happiness.

Shortly after Nick's death, my heart was lifted by a random "God thing." My brother Richard—whom I had not been close to for years—and I found ourselves visiting our mom at the same time. We had a wonderful heart-to-heart conversation, and we committed to moving forward in reconciliation from that day on. I felt elated!

One month later, heartbreak struck again. Shockingly, Richard and his wife, Jan, died in a terrible car accident. They were killed instantly. I had a very difficult time wrapping my head and heart around that. One of the hardest things I've ever done was to take my mother in her wheelchair to say goodbye to her son and daughter-in-law. I was dealing with my grief and feeling hers as well. It was beyond words.

Approximately six months after Nick's, Richard's, and Jan's passing, Mom died at her home with friends, family, and Faith Hospice by her side. We were getting together that day to celebrate my birthday. She had taken a turn for the worse that morning before I arrived. Our friend Kathy, mom's caregiver, noticed she wasn't doing well, but she was a very strong woman and had bounced back so many times before. I was sure some nourishment and a festive atmosphere would work in her favor. She was, after all, my mom—my rock, my inspiration. She wasn't going to die. What would I do without her? We were always together, and now I was on my own. But, no, God was right there every step of the way.

After the funeral, it seemed I went on "autopilot." A few months had gone by, and Janet, Faith Hospice's grief counselor, called to ask how I was doing and wondered if I would like to come in to talk. I thanked her and said, "No, I'm fine." She gave me her number, and I put it away.

In the coming months, I noticed I was racing around, starting projects and not finishing them. I was forgetting things, which was scary to me. Also, my half-brother, Bob, had been battling cancer, and he passed away. My heart was broken, as we didn't get a chance to see each other much. He was one of those guys who was a joy to be around, very down-to-earth, and real. I couldn't attend the funeral because I was out of town. That deepened my sadness.

Shortly after Bob passed away, my sister-in-law, Pat, passed from cancer after being sick for a few short months. We shared so many great family moments. Once, we were on Family Feud together with Nick's mom, dad, and sister-in-law Barb. I have great memories of this wonderful woman. I miss her. During this time, all I could think was, "When is this going to stop? I simply cannot lose another loved one!"

One day, shortly after Pat's passing, I was out for a few hours and came home to find that my beloved Angel, our Bichon Friese, had passed. She had suffered from diabetes for two years. Angel's death was devastating because when Nick brought her home, I didn't want a dog, yet she became glued to me and followed me everywhere. She sure got me through some very difficult times, and I was grieving yet again for another family member whom I loved dearly.

Soon after Angel's death, I decided I could probably benefit from some counseling. I wasn't comfortable with grief groups, but I did pray about it. I called Janet at Faith Hospice. A year after my time with Janet, I began remembering things a lot better and making progress in accomplishing things—basically, feeling much more grounded. I joined a Bible study, got a job, and started going out dancing occasionally with my girlfriends.

Is my life back to normal? Not in the slightest! But I have a new normal. I have a wonderful support system of family and friends and anticipate a future of enjoying my children and grandchildren and simply living my life to the fullest. I allow myself to grieve for each of my loved ones, especially when the "waves" come and moving forward involves a lot of curves. One of my favorite Bible verses is Psalm 23, which has provided me with much solace and peace. When I need strength, I turn to Psalm 23 and read it, praying over it until it refreshes my soul.

Psalm 23, A Psalm of David.

The LORD is my shepherd, I shall not be in want. He makes me lie down in green pastures, he leads me beside quiet waters, he restores my soul. He guides me in paths of righteousness for his name's sake. Even though I walk through the valley of the shadow of death, I will fear no evil, for you are with me; your rod and your staff, they comfort me. You prepare a table before me in the presence of my enemies. You anoint my head with oil; my cup overflows. Surely goodness and love will follow me all the days of my life, and I will dwell in the house of the LORD forever (NIV).

Thank you, my dear children—Amy, Aaron, and Tyler—for walking this grief journey together.

My Grief Journey: Laura Alley Hoekstra

In Loving Memory
Robert Bruce Hoekstra 1.16.1957–8.16.2000 Husband/Father
Janet Elaine Alley 3.31.1935–3.11.2013 Mother/Grandmother
Harvey Winton Alley 12.10.1925–5.7.2020 Father/Grandfather

> **The People in Israel Have the Wailing Wall.**
> **I've Had the Wailing Tub.**

Starting in the year 2000, I experienced a series of major losses. They have been life-altering and painful. I've thrice wondered how to carry on. One thing I have discovered: a safe place for grieving is of vital, undeniable importance. Let me share mine with you.

The Wailing Tub

My husband, Bob, died at the age of forty-three, three months after a bilateral lung transplant. Overnight, I became the busy single parent of a toddler, continuing my work as an IT training manager for a Fortune 100 company in the Chicago area. My days were long. After commuting, working, supper, play, bath, and bedtime stories, I was exhausted. More often than not, once Betsy, our two-year-old, was asleep, I filled up the bathtub, turned on some music, and soaked while the tears spilled down my cheeks into the water. Perhaps it was the scent of the bubbles, reminding me of Bob's long tub baths after his transplant surgery, or maybe it was the healing worship songs from the CD given to us during his lengthy illness. Or it could have been the droning exhaust fan offering me the freedom to wail. And wail I did. There were times I gave myself a bloody nose, the crying jags were that intense. I could hear the groans and moans coming from my throat, along with one-word prayers consisting of "Jesus . . . Jesus . . . Jeee—sus." Had an observer watched, they might have believed I was losing my mind, possibly even a danger to myself.

For much of the time, I kept my tears inside so I could function in my world of serving as an employee, manager, mama, and friend. But once I was alone, I could not hold them back. The flowered wallpaper in my bathroom began to peel away from the walls' edges, soaked from the humid air that was filled with steam and tears. The wailing tub was my refuge.

The Car

The year 2011 found me in a new season of life—the sandwich years. Betsy was in middle school when my mom was stricken with multiple myeloma. Both of my parents were living, but my mom was the healthier one, and her illness caught us all off-guard. My siblings were unavailable and Mom's physical and emotional needs were intense. Caregiving, while parenting and working full time, demanded more than I had to give, but I had no options. Watching my parents decline during this time brought its own deep sorrow. My car became a safe place for grieving the impending loss.

Adding to my normal daily demands—taking my mom back and forth to chemo treatments, making occasional emergency room visits, and visiting a rehab facility when she was too weak to return home after a hospitalization—these trips became routine and expected. Once again, tears came when I found myself alone, listening to music, driving through McDonald's for yogurt parfaits and iced tea, and sitting outside the church or school when picking Betsy up from her activities. Napkins are no substitute for facial tissue, but I used what was within reach. In the end, Mom's last days were spent at Trillium Woods, an almost thirty-minute drive from home. I sobbed freely each time I left her, fogging up the windows while my eyes glazed red and puffy. Traveling that stretch of highway still triggers those memories.

Zoom Meetings

In May of 2020, my dad took his final breaths at Trillium Woods after years of living with heart disease and congestive heart failure. Because of the COVID-19 pandemic, we were not able to celebrate his life with loved ones and friends. We had a graveside service, limited to ten people plus the officiant. We were masked and distanced according to our family units; Betsy was unable to return from college. I was alone in my home and isolated from friends and church. As for my grieving spaces? The wailing tub reappeared, the car was occasionally used, but now the hallowed space known as Zoom entered my life.

I was now an orphaned, widowed empty nester. Family relationships had become strained during the years of caregiving due to a lack of real and honest communication with my siblings. Grief and isolation swept over me like an icy cold wave. Feeling the weight and pressure of my dad's final months and the lack of family support, my doctor approved a medical leave of absence from my job, treating me for depression and anxiety. In desperation, I also reached out to Faith Hospice and asked for support. I was quickly given a virtual appointment with a caring and compassionate bereavement counselor. Because of the pandemic, we met regularly via Zoom over the next year. She spent hours listening, encouraging, offering wise words, helping me process my grief. As I talked, my head became clearer and my heart began to experience peace and restoration. Who knew Zoom would become my next place of grieving?

The Faithfulness of God

In all of my grieving places, despite feeling desolate and abandoned, I have never really been alone. At times, my feelings overshadow my trust and faith in God. The hurt and loneliness I have experienced in the throes of loss continue to be exposed and excised with the help of my faith community and the love of friends. I have deep compassion for human suffering that has grown more urgent with the ongoing pandemic. Because God has been faithful to me through my tears and life losses, I have committed to work and serve as a hospice volunteer and end-of-life doula. The time I have spent in my "grieving places" allows me to recognize and enter into the grieving spaces of others. For me, being fully alive includes embracing the reality of death and offering gifts of care, comfort, and presence on the journey. I cannot think of a better way to live.

My Grief Journey: Allison Moores

*(written at age twelve, adapted from article first published in **GirlStory** magazine)*

> ### *Empty Chair*

What is loss? Loss is "the harm or privation resulting from losing or being separated from someone or something." That is the definition of loss in the Merriam-Webster dictionary. But what is the reality of processing this experience? At the time, it can feel as if all that you have is being stripped away from you, your mind and heart left as hollow, sunken holes where something used to be. An aching pulse that runs you through and through, shaking you from the top of your head to the tip of your toes, seeming like it lasts forever.

I lay in bed. It's Christmas Eve. Like any other child, I lie awake in hopes to shoot up when Santa crawls through that chimney, tiptoes over to the tree, and lays his presents down one by one. Maybe I can catch him! Maybe he will take me away to a magical world, add even more bliss to my life. But of course, sleep takes over the passions of a five-year-old. In the morning, I run over to the tree to see all of my presents. I missed him! I look over at my parents, a huge smile plastered on my face. They seem unhappy. It's Christmas, so I can't think of a reason why. I turn back over and peel the wrapping paper off of my new present, with not a care in the world besides finding out what lies underneath the wrapping paper—certainly not what lies in my parents' heads, the reason they are upset on the happiest day of the year.

After a day filled with laughter and joy, I pull the warm blanket over my head and cuddle with my new toys. I had completely forgotten to ask why my parents seemed upset! It probably doesn't matter. The next morning, I wake up, ready to play with my new toys, read a book, draw, or do whatever the day holds. I grab a book and fall onto my mom's couch. I can hardly focus, but I calm myself by dissecting the words. I am in *Land of Stories*, laughing through the woods with the main characters, Alex and Connor. Suddenly, BOOM! The evil queen pops out of the tree.

"Allison?" She doesn't say this menacingly, it sounds as if she is crying. I realize it's not the evil queen. I close my book and look over to see my mom sitting on the edge of the couch. "Sweetie,

there's something I need to tell you. Yesterday, your brother . . ."
she chokes on the words. I look at her confused, my eyes pleading
that what I think will be said isn't true. Deep inside, I realize why
my parents were not themselves yesterday. "Your brother Alex . .
. he was driving to the beach to see his friends. His tire caught on
the curb of the road, and . . . he was . . . he . . ." I look down, conflicted. I feel as if a punch has been thrown through my heart. The
tears on my face feel like hot lava burning through my skin. My
head pounds, and I wonder if the world has stopped, or at least
has been slowed to this one deafeningly quiet moment.

I close my eyes and try to escape back into my book.

I am skipping through the forest, when . . . BOOM! The queen
pops out of the tree, her minions behind her. Alex from the *Land
of Stories* smiles at me, reassuringly. Her face changes from hers to
Alex's, my brother's. Why do they have to have the same name?
The tree's cracks and curves turn into agonized faces. They say my
name. Anywhere I look, I am slowly dragged back to reality. When
I am pulled through, it hits me like a bullet, the sounds ringing
in my ears. This is what loss must feel like. A punch through the
heart, hot lava burning the face, a pounding in the head. It feels
as if you are punched through like a hole puncher through paper.
The pieces ripped from you are still somewhere. They exist maybe
in another universe, or even in the past, a second ago, before this
has all happened.

However, the holes can never grow back. You cannot tape
them back to the paper. You can try, but one day or another, the
glossy tape gets in the way of the space you have on that paper, of
the beautiful and imperfect expanding artwork that is your soul.
All you can do is do your best to cope, to patch up those holes
with new memories and experiences, to bring new people into
your life. You can't try and distract yourself by throwing yourself

back into another story, another piece of imagination. You must deal with what is in front of you, no matter how painful it may be. There will always be tomorrow to doze off. Instead of making a story in your head to distract yourself from what is right in front of you, focus on expanding your piece of art. It works not by moving around the huge holes, or even with tiny scratches, but by building something new and wonderful above them, your memories as the solid foundation. I miss my brother, but I am finally finding my voice and the ability to talk about him. That is what loss means to me. Not the feeling of it, but what can come after.

My Grief Journey: Cynthia Kay

I was not in Raleigh when my mom passed away. I was not in Clearwater Beach when my father passed away. In both cases, I had been there days before, but my parents, I believe, "decided" to wait until I went back to Michigan before going home to the Lord.

My parents Ann and Gus Afendoulis each gave me many special gifts. My mother gave me the gift of creativity. She was a musician, amateur artist, and creative thinker. To Mom, all things were possible. And believe me, she could convince anyone to do anything. She was a force. Dad was a businessman but not the kind you might think of when you hear that word. He was a man who would co-sign loans for employees. He would go back to the store at night because someone forgot to pick up their cleaning and needed a suit for the next day. He would give away dry-cleaning to a never-ending line of nonprofits. He was also an accomplished bridge player, a life master. My success as a media professional and business owner is due, in no small part, to the confidence, creativity, and competence I gained from them.

That is not to say that it was always wonderful. My mom could be difficult, to say the least, and she was not always pleased with me. But, as my sister would often say, "You are Mom's favorite, which is why she is so hard on you." By the way, my sister and brother were also favorites but in different ways.

When my parents retired and moved away to sunny Florida, it was such a joy. They had arthritis and the warm weather suited them. I made lots of trips to Florida over the years, and when they reached the point they could not be alone, my sister and I gave them a choice. They needed to be close to one of us, in Raleigh, North Carolina or Grand Rapids, Michigan. In the words of my father Gus, "I'm no fool; Michigan is cold." And so they moved to Raleigh to be close to my sister and her family.

As Mom's health declined, my sister kept telling me I did not need to come to help. She would tell me when she needed me. She never did, even though she and her husband were running a business, working ridiculous hours, and caring for my parents. That is why seven months before my mom passed, I just surprised them—showed up one weekend and made a promise to my sister. I would be there every month to give them a break. She did not argue. The trips were emotionally draining. Every time I left, I cried. Honestly, I felt guilty that I was not there more, even though my sister assured me that was not the case.

When I suggested hospice, my sister was somewhat surprised. She was there every day and so the decline was more obvious to me. An assessment showed that Mom needed hospice. Hospice brought us an immediate sense of relief. The care and concern for the entire family were a blessing. They knew what to expect and helped us understand that what we were experiencing and feeling were not uncommon. They were emotionally supportive when we were unsure of the path forward. They made the journey less frightening and helped us practically deal with the inevitable.

The last time I was there, my mom sat with me on the couch all day with a faraway look in her eyes, holding my hand, not saying a word. When I put her to bed, I told her I was leaving early in the morning. She looked up and clearly said, "I think you should." Mom passed away a few days later. I always told myself that I wanted to be sure to do everything I could for Mom and Dad. I did not want to have regrets. It might sound odd that I did not have regrets but still felt guilty. Did I do enough to help my sister's family? They carried a huge burden and did so without ever complaining. Did I listen enough? Did I thank them enough for caring for our parents?

In times of trial, it is faith that sustains me. Honestly, I struggle to understand how people face the death of a loved one without faith. I am fortunate to have a church family and friends that stepped up. Funerals in the Greek Orthodox church are healing. The hymns, the prayers, the traditions. Two phrases cut right to the core. We say, "*memory eternal.*" We don't move on. We remember. We also greet each other with "Life to us." This is to remind us that while our loved one is gone, we must continue to live.

In our church, we do memorial services for our loved ones after forty days, one year, five years, and then at various intervals. They are like mini-funerals. When we did Mom's forty-day memorial, I reached a milestone. I felt some peace. And with Mom gone, we needed to turn our attention to Dad. He did well for a time. He loved to sing in the choir, and into his nineties, he was still singing. He would go with his grandson every week to church unless the choir was not singing. Then his favorite line was "No choir, no church." After sixty-seven years of singing, I think he deserved a break now and then. But he was always on time when the choir was singing and berated the young latecomers. He would say, "If I can get to church at my age on time, you have no excuse."

In 2017, he had a stroke and could not live alone. By this time, my sister and her husband had sold their business. The three of them moved to Florida and lived together. At first, Dad was excited, but he soon discovered that so much had changed in Florida in the years since he had last been there. One day, he said, "We don't have many friends here anymore." It was heartbreaking.

Every night, at the same time, I would call my dad. It was common knowledge among my friends and even customers that no matter where I was, I would excuse myself to call him. He could not go to sleep without hearing from me. He still worried about me, especially when I was traveling. As his health declined even further, I started making more frequent trips to Florida. Each time I visited, he thanked me, as if I was doing something extraordinary. And every night he would say, "Thank you", when my sister put him to bed. Every morning, he would wake up and say, "Thank you, God, for one more day." Now, I do that as well. It has become a morning ritual.

Soon my sister and brother-in-law could not even leave the house for a short time. They took turns running errands, and friends had to come over to my father's home for visits. This time, we knew exactly what to do. Once again, we called on hospice, and within about six months, dad passed away. Once again, the support was amazing.

The grief you feel when you lose your first parent is multiplied 100-fold when you lose the remaining parent. The first several months after Dad passed away, I would instinctively pick up the phone every night to call him. At first, it upset me. I knew he had died. Why was this happening? Then I decided it was a sign. I was still connected to him, and he would always be here. That is why faith is so important. We believe in life after death. We believe that our loved ones are in a better place.

My Grief Journey: Jennifer Feuerstein

> ### A Decade of Loss

Grief took hold of my heart during a ten-year period where the losses through death mounted one on top of another—nine times. It was suffocating. Heart-wrenching. Traumatic. But as I journeyed in life further away from the grief, I healed. God had separated me from the pain through time. The journey forever changed me as a person but carved me into the woman I am today.

My first walk with death was when I lost my beloved grandmother, Valerie, when I was twenty. She was old and sick for a long time, so it wasn't unexpected. But it was *unexperienced*. I had never lost someone close to me, and I wasn't familiar with the grief process. It was the first time I ever felt such depths of sadness. And though people would offer condolences, that did little to comfort me. What did help was sharing stories about her. The laughter and joy in commemorating her life allowed this cold, barren experience of death to cover me in a warm blanket of familiarity. Her death, as awful as it felt, couldn't prepare me for what lay ahead though.

After my husband and I had our first child, we were excited to grow our family. We got pregnant with our second, and I miscarried. It was Mother's Day weekend, and the irony felt cruel. We weren't prepared for this to be our story. It hurt. *A lot.* After we shed a waterfall of tears, we regained confidence that we'd have more children to complete our family portrait. Yet, the next three pregnancies all resulted in miscarriages as well. Each one became more soul-crushing to experience because our hope and confidence dissolved further and further. The loss of our babies on top of the loss of hope that we'd have more children was mind-numbing. It was over six years that we lost four pregnancies to miscarriage. Each time, a flame of hope would flicker with the positive test result, and it would be snuffed out with the inevitable miscarriage.

Then I got pregnant a fifth time. This time, the pregnancy didn't end as a result of a miscarriage. Instead, we discovered it was an ectopic pregnancy. The embryo had implanted itself in my fallopian tube, and if the tube ruptured, it could kill me. I was rushed to the hospital to have emergency surgery to remove the unviable pregnancy. The surgeon performed the procedure that would save my life but not my baby's. It was devastating to think I may never have more children. Through counseling, my therapist helped me reframe the family portrait I had envisioned. I would have to come to peace with the reality that it might include only one child.

During the same six-year period, two cousins (tragically on the same side of the family), Jeannine and Sarah, were diagnosed with cancer. Jeannine died after a short battle at the age of twenty-nine. Sarah died less than two years later. She fought hard but succumbed to the disease at the age of twenty-eight. I clearly remember the day Sarah died. I had a doctor's appointment earlier in the day where I was informed yet again that I wasn't pregnant. Grief overtook me as I returned to Sarah's bedside at the hospital. We were extremely close, and I was there holding her hand as she took her last breath. She had suffered so greatly; I knew her passing would end her suffering. But it only intensified mine.

The final blow came two years later with the unexpected death of my lifelong best friend, Julie. Julie and I were like sisters.

Closer than sisters. We had been inseparable for our entire lives. She died suddenly and tragically of a pulmonary embolism at the age of thirty. I was pummeled. My already battered heart experienced inexplicable anguish. I still remember lying in bed for days, unable to move. The cumulative losses depleted my life energy, and I couldn't function. I don't know how I managed to survive the early days of Julie's death—the entire decade of death that was permeating my life. I was wiped out from so much darkness. This season of death was like walking through thick tar and black fog. I wasn't sure if I'd ever find my way out of the intense darkness.

I experienced wave after wave of grief for ten years. The waves seemed to crash closer and closer, and it was difficult to catch my breath. I felt like I was drowning in a sea of death.

And then I received my first glimmer of light in the darkness. I had learned I was pregnant a few days before Julie's death. For whatever reason, this pregnancy would be successful. We welcomed our second child. I never miscarried again and successfully had a third child. They are my miracle babies. I saw light emerge in the darkness and each day, the light got a little brighter.

It's now been eighteen years since Julie's death and the end of the decade of death. I don't know why I had to walk this path of excruciating grief. I'll never understand it on this side of Heaven. What got me through, though, was God. If I didn't have my faith to cling to, I wouldn't have recovered fully from the pain. I had people praying for me and over me. I sought spiritual direction to keep me afloat. I prayed prayers that had no words, sometimes only sobbing, knowing every tear was bottled up by God and that He held me when I couldn't breathe.

Each experience of death was vastly different. But I remember the pain being the same. I felt so alone, even as I stood alongside others who were also grieving. Grief is a solo journey—making it an isolating one. But it's with God. I know God was there every step of the way. God healed me and time separated me from the raw pain. There was no instant cure for the pain, though. The wounds healed slowly and then somewhere along the way, I didn't hurt so much. I don't know when my heart healed, but it did. And I've now been through enough loss in life to know that I won't ever stay in that place of pain. Somewhere and somehow, God will heal me again.

My Grief Journey: Buck Matthews

The Death of My First Hero

I was fourteen when the battlefield gas of World War I finally took my father down. He was fifty-four and the center of my life. His death at a VA hospital in Washington, DC was probably not a surprise to my mother, who knew how seriously ill he was. To me, it was a shock because I didn't. Worse, before anyone could intervene, I saw his rolled-up mattress and his sheeted figure being wheeled away.

Ours was a close and caring family, and my mother was courageous in keeping her grief from taking us down. I reacted as I thought I should, playing the role of the man in the family, hiding the cavernous hole in my heart as he was interred with honors at Arlington National Cemetery.

I didn't cry. Not that day or that week or even that month. I felt guilty. Then one day, three months after his funeral, I came home from school, lay down on my bed, and sobbed for five hours. My mother, who must have wondered at my seeming indifference to losing my hero, had the wisdom not to interfere. We didn't speak of it the following day, but we all knew that it was a good and healing thing.

I was a young teenager, but death was not a mystery to me. We'd lost other family members in earlier years. I understood that one day, they just weren't there anymore. But I didn't know anything about how to grieve, and nobody else knew how to guide a child through it. There were no Five Stages for kids. There still aren't.

When I think about this, I think about how great a burden grief is for a surviving parent, who must do what my mother did—allow me to process it my own way. It probably wasn't the best way, and the outcome could have been unfavorable.

There may never be a right way to help children deal with the loss of the important people in their lives. But we should never presume they get over it more easily than adults.

My Grief Journey: Ann Webb

When peace like a river attendeth my way, when sorrows like sea billows roll. Whatever my lot, Thou hast taught me to say, it is well, it is well with my soul.

"It Is Well With My Soul" by hymnist Horatio Spafford

and composer Philip Bliss.

> ### *The Passing of My Beloved Mother*

As a child, I had a recurring nightmare that my mother had died. I would wake with tears streaming down my cheeks, followed by an intense sense of relief. *It was just a dream.*

I have been keenly aware for the majority of my life that one of my greatest sources of heartache would be the loss of my mother, and then, this heartache started to materialize right before my eyes. I sat for days with my mother as she slowly and deliberately completed her time on earth. What a roller coaster of emotions, from the deep ache of knowing my time with her on earth was ending, to a sense of impatience with the grueling deathwatch process, to immense guilt for the impatience of wanting the process to end, to regret because I could have been a better daughter, to relief that her suffering would end, to an all-consuming sadness that I would soon face life without the comfort of her sweet, gentle smile.

Looking back, I now realize the process had started long before I was ready to accept that my mother was in her last months on earth. She slowly withdrew from conversations, was no longer particular about keeping her hair combed, and spent much of her day napping in her chair.

My mission became keeping her healthy, prolonging the inevitable. After all, she had conquered ovarian cancer at eighty-nine; she was a survivor. I saw her on a daily basis, incorporating her bedtime routine into my visits and overseeing as many aspects of her care as I was able.

Enter COVID-19 and our routine was turned upside-down as I was no longer allowed access to the facility where she had lived for the last nine years of her life. I became irrationally angry with the virus, the governor for locking down assisted living facilities, and the staff at her facility because they were able to see her and care for her when I couldn't. I barked orders from outside her window—her hair wasn't combed; her bedsore slippers weren't positioned correctly on her feet; she needed a pillow between her knees. I told myself the restricted visitation would only last a couple of weeks, but the lockdown dragged on and on as I helplessly watched the natural progression of the end of her life from the outside.

Fortunately, I had made arrangements for hospice care shortly before the pandemic. How kind and patient they were with me as I battled the reality of the inevitable and agonized that I couldn't be there to help care for her. Holding her hand and saying our nightly prayers together were things I had taken for granted.

By the grace of God and the help of her hospice nurse, a bed was secured at a residential hospice facility. I was allowed unlimited time to be with her and could even spend the night. Her placement was the result of a Kennedy terminal ulcer that appeared just above her tail bone, a dark sore that develops rapidly during the final stages of life. I pushed back this reality to a place that was safe from any conscious consideration and instead, rejoiced in our reunion. I explained the magnitude of the pandemic and watched her eyes widen with amazement, but I couldn't bring myself to tell her that she was in a hospice facility, convinced she would think I had given up on her. Within a day, she became unresponsive, but I continued to insist she was offered meals, convinced she had to eat and recover.

My mother had a dear Christian friend from church that visited faithfully for several years as part of an outreach program. Terra had come to love my mother; they shared an instant connection and a love for the Lord. I confided in Terra about my fear of telling Mom that she was in a hospice facility, and the kindness and wisdom in Terra's response marked a turning point in my understanding and acceptance of her end-of-life journey. I needed to tell my mother she was soon going to see Jesus, God's promise to her would be fulfilled. Terra's words helped me realize my fierce determination to keep my mom alive was more for me than her.

My mother was ready, but I was not.

Over the last few months, her body had deteriorated to the point she was unable to roll over in bed or feed herself. Any ability to care for herself had slipped away, and the pain of even small adjustments in her position had become excruciating. It was clear to me that I needed to reassure her that because of her example, I had become a strong and competent woman. I would be alright, but oh, how I would miss her. John 16:22 says, "And ye now therefore have sorrow: but I will see you again, and your heart shall rejoice, and your joy no man taketh from you" (KJV). I prayed I would find the words that conveyed the deep love I felt and the confidence that, although her life on earth was ending, she would soon be in Heaven.

My mother had shared with me her fear that she might not be worthy of Heaven. Although it was hard for me to fathom this pure and genuine Christian woman would harbor this fear, my words had to be reassuring that her Christian faith and love for the Lord would be rewarded in Heaven. Ephesians 2:8 (ESV)—"For by grace you have been saved through faith. And this is not your own doing; it is the gift of God . . ."—spoke to those fears. I held her hand, tears streaming down my cheeks, as I told her about the glory she would soon experience. To this day, I am relieved that she was unresponsive during the conversation, yet I know with all of my being that she heard and understood my words.

On May 16, 2020, at 8:46 a.m., my precious mother took her last breath of life and slipped peacefully into the arms of her Heavenly Father. I was sitting next to her, holding her hand in a surreal yet undeniable understanding that the end was near. And then, her breathing peacefully stopped. I sat quietly, consumed with a deep physical ache throughout my being, yet also wrapped in a sense of relief. Such a contradiction of emotions. She went to Heaven with all the grace and dignity she portrayed throughout her ninety-five years of life. This quiet woman of great faith now knew firsthand the gift of eternal life.

Praise God, she had arrived.

Grief comes in waves and can be overwhelming and paralyzing. Although there are times I can anticipate a wave of sorrow, it can also present itself at the most unexpected, and sometimes inconvenient, times. Yet throughout my continuing journey of sorrow and grief, I always find great comfort in knowing my mother is in Heaven. I thank God for my faith and pray for those that face the sting of death without the belief that death is not the end, only the beginning. Although my mother had an unconditional and unwavering love for her family and her life, she wouldn't choose to return. The greatest gift I received from my mother was the message of salvation and the Christian faith she instilled through her example. She is singing God's praises, and I will join her someday. Until then, I thank my God upon every remembrance of you, Mom. "When we've been there ten thousand years, bright shining as the sun, we've no less days to sing God's praise than when we first begun!" ("Amazing Grace").

My Grief Journey: Paula Jauch

> ### *My Parents Died Way Too Young*

When I lost my parents, it was confusing for me. Looking back now, years later, I can see why. I had to go through several grieving processes. As a child, I grew up in addiction where there was a lot of abuse and neglect. When my parents were dying, I had mixed emotions swirling inside me. What I didn't know at the time was that I was feeling conflicted. I knew I was going to lose them, but I also knew, deep down inside, I had already lost them years ago to their addictions.

One night, when my mother was really sick and lying in her bed, I rested my head on her stomach as I knelt at her bedside. The moment my head came in contact with her stomach, I started to weep bitterly. At the time, I didn't fully know what was going on; I just felt deep sorrow. Looking back now, after many years of trauma therapy, I know I was grieving the loss of my mother before she had even left this earth. I was grieving the mother I always wanted and the mother I never had. She was only given a few months to live at this time. In my head, I wanted to fix the situation, but I didn't even know what needed to be fixed.

The other day, one of my favorite Bible teachers spoke these words, "I loved my parents because they were my parents, but I didn't have the love you would have toward a nurturing parent." I was in the middle of my workout at the time. When I heard these words, I had to stop and go write them down. I told myself *that's it.* Those were the words I needed to hear to explain how I have felt about my parents all along. Right before losing both of my parents, I was in the process of healing from a lot of childhood trauma, and what I didn't realize until later is that when my parents passed away, I had already grieved the loss of them.

The Loss of My Parents

Losing a parent can feel very confusing at first. In the beginning, you want to do whatever you can to try to make them better—sometimes to the point of denying what is really going on. You will see this a lot when others are losing loved ones as well. The doctors try their best to give you a timeline and tell you what their recommendations are for your parent. For many people, this provokes anger when they say your mom only has about a month left—if that. Most people are not ready to lose a parent, so they usually take this information as offensive and toss it out the window. I know that is how most of my siblings and I reacted to the news. Not to mention, a lot of us were trying to make decisions out of childhood wounds that had not been healed.

My mother's cancer started in her cervix and then spread throughout her body. Once it hit her lungs, she was having trouble breathing and needed fluid drained from her lungs daily. My siblings and I all have a strong faith, so we were believing for God to heal her. My mom was not ready to go. She had six children and twenty-four grandchildren at the time. But there came a point where I knew things were heading in another direction. There was a lot of chaos going on around my mother in her room. Everyone wanted to make sure she had her last wishes fulfilled. She was asking for all types of food that she couldn't eat because her body was getting so frail and shutting down.

She spent about a month in the hospital, and then my siblings and I tried to bring her home to my brother's house. This only lasted for about five days because it required caring for her 24/7: an oxygen tank, a pain pump, and a full list of medications that we were not prepared to handle. We tried our best to take care of her, but we finally realized this was not the best option for my mother's circumstances because her health was declining so quickly.

I'll never forget when I got the call from my brother that they were moving my mom to hospice. This information hit me hard. I remember running into the bathroom and falling on my knees and just sobbing. There were so many things I still wanted to say and do with my mom, and I felt she was just too young to die.

Looking back now, I remember everyone handled it so differently. I eventually got to the point where I knew we needed to make a change. Amid the turmoil I was feeling, I snuck off into a side room to call my pastor to get some advice. The only words he spoke to me were, "You hear from God. You will know what to do."

After I got off that phone call, one of the nurses taking care of my mom walked by me and asked if she could talk to me. She said we needed to make my mom more comfortable by upping her meds. This is where a lot of people have a hard time. But after losing both my parents to cancer in hospice, I now understand this is part of the process. It's necessary to increase pain relief medications so they no longer have to suffer here on earth.

I lost my mom in 2007 and my father in 2016 to cancer. The experience of losing my mother made me a little more prepared for when I lost my father. When my father was dying, I observed the same things going on with my siblings. Everyone heading in different directions, each with their own opinions about what they thought we should be doing with my dad. One sibling even recommended we take him home and out of hospice.

Again, this is the time I felt I needed to step in. My words to my siblings were that we needed to put our feelings aside and do what was best for Dad. He was sick, suffering. We all needed to spend as much time as we could with him, and if they had anything to say to him, they should say it then. I felt this was an important lesson, which I had learned when we lost our mom.

Before my father's passing, I got to spend a few nights with him in hospice. It wasn't very comfortable because hospice didn't have a place for me to sleep. But it gave me peace and comfort knowing I was with him in his last days. I said everything I felt I needed to say to him—the best I knew how to say it at the time.

There was a lot I needed to forgive my father for, but I was grateful that I was in trauma therapy at the time. The last words I spoke to my father were, "No matter what you did to me, I never stopped loving you."

If I could leave anyone with a piece of advice as their loved ones are passing, it is this: put your faith and hope in the Lord. I know it is not easy losing a loved one. And no one is ever prepared for it. But I encourage you to put your trust in God and know you will see your loved one again someday. Leave no words upspoken, and if you need to forgive yourself or another person, ask God to help you.

"Trust in the Lord with all thine heart; and lean not unto thine own understanding. In all your way acknowledge Him, and He shall direct thy paths" (Proverbs 3:5–6, KJV).

My Grief Journey: Kim Johnson

> ### *My Life Turned Upside-down in 2020*

My phone rang at 2:16 a.m. on June 30, 2020, waking me up from a sound sleep. I got up to answer it and saw on the caller ID that it was my mom's phone number. She was only right upstairs; I knew something was wrong.

I picked up the phone and said hello. At first, I heard nothing, so I said, "Mom? Are you there?" Finally, in a winded voice, she said, "I think I need to go to the hospital. I'm having trouble breathing."

By the time I had gotten upstairs, she was up and headed for the living room. I led her to a chair, and I picked up the phone to call 911. I did not want to take the chance of something happening with me driving her to the hospital.

Once we arrived at the hospital, they immediately took her back to a room and sent me to the waiting room to be screened since we were in the throngs of the COVID-19 pandemic. The wait seemed like forever, and I got my phone out, putting a plea on my Facebook page for anyone who was still awake to please pray because I was in the ER with my mom. We were not sure what was wrong. I was grateful that two people responded, telling me they were praying and to keep them posted.

About an hour later, they called me back to see my mom. Before I went into the room, the attending doctor took me aside and asked how long my mom had cancer. I almost fainted. Having a hard time responding, I finally said, "She doesn't!"

The X-rays they showed us were devastating, revealing that her lungs were full of tumors and a large mass the size of a navel orange on her breastbone sat close to her heart. After many tests and biopsies, it was revealed that my mom, unknowingly, had stage 4 metastatic breast cancer.

We were given the even more devastating news that even with chemotherapy, she may only live six months to a year. After only one treatment, my sweet mother succumbed to the wicked cancer, only twenty days after that ER visit. We had zero time to prepare. My mom and I never really talked about it—she chose not to. She did tell a visiting pastor, who she spoke with when I was not there, that she was not worried about herself. She was worried about me, her only child. What was going to happen to her baby when she was gone, the one she loved so much?

Before she passed away, we did have a brief heart-to-heart about what to do with the house and other things . . . the appointments she had scheduled, the bank deposits.

I remember saying to her, "Mom, I don't want you to leave me, but I don't want you to suffer, and right now, you are suffering." It was true. She was clearly uncomfortable and suffering, fighting to breathe as her body shut down.

On the day she died, at 1 p.m., another pastor had arrived to pray over her and for me. She opened her eyes, and I said to her. "Are you ready to go home? I mean home with Jesus?"

She nodded her head yes. "Then go ahead and go home. I will be okay."

I think that was the permission she needed and the comfort she wanted to experience—that I was going to be okay without her. So at 3:15 p.m. that afternoon, my mom took her last breath with me whispering praise songs over her, singing her into the arms of Jesus.

The pastor who was there with me let me stand there, looking at my mom for only a few minutes, then she led me gently out of the room. Later, I learned that my mom had instructed the pastor to make sure I left, not wanting me to stick around, looking at her body.

I drove home and called a few friends to let them know that my mom was gone. Many came to be with me; one was aware of the book my mom had left for me: *For After I am Gone.* My mom had put this book together a few years before, one that had her wishes, the deed to the house, all of her life insurance policies with her funeral requests outlined, and cemetery arrangements that she had pre-planned and already paid for. The only thing I had to buy was her headstone. She wanted a closed casket, and she wanted everyone out of the cemetery before they lowered the casket.

Next came the loneliness. With the funeral over, people returned to their lives. I knew that my friends would be there in a heartbeat if I asked, but with the COVID-19 restrictions, it was difficult asking for help. But one last wish from my mom was to sell our home of forty-seven years and move.

It was the home she and I shared since 1973, and I was to put it up for sale. Forty-seven years of memories, love, and even scents— the only home I knew. I closed off my mom's room because I could not bear to go in there. When I did, all I smelled was her, and it crushed my heart. I asked two of my mom's friends to clear out her room because I could not do it. It took nearly twenty of my friends and me, friends who would come over in the evenings and weekends, and within two months, we had the entire home's contents either packed up into storage, given away, or donated to charity. My home was sold within twenty-four hours of being listed. I said goodbye to the place that held forty-seven years of our lives on October 24, 2020. I felt sad, still numb from everything that had happened in the last four months.

Once I moved, I took some more time off from work and finally grieved. I crumbled. I kept hearing from people that I wasn't alone, that God was there, and that He would be more than enough. But most of the people who kept telling me that were those who may have lost someone close but also had a family to support them; I did not. For me, at that time anyway, God was not enough. I felt so alone. I felt betrayed by this God who claimed to love me. "How can a God of love let something like this happen? Let my mom die . . . and so quickly?" I was angry at God, which many of my friends told me I had no business feeling. Some said I should never be mad at God and told me I was engaging in a cardinal sin. Yeah, well maybe I was, but I didn't care.

Christmas came that year, and it was so difficult to get through, I had been involved in a Grief Share group but because of COVID restrictions, we met on Zoom. It was doable but felt so impersonal, especially when I was feeling so isolated in the first place.

I was working from home, attending church from home, and now grieving with others from home. I had a couple of friends come over and decorate my new house because I just couldn't do it. My mom was one of those people who went all out with decorating and loved and looked forward to the new innovative ideas I would come up with. She wasn't there to do this with me now.

I had a friend who lost both of her parents within a short period tell me, "Trust me and believe me when I say, you won't always be this distraught." To me, I saw no light at the end of the tunnel as I cried daily while pining for my sweet momma. The hurt was deep, and it was real. The anger at God, and those telling me that everything was going to be okay—to just put it in God's hands—was fierce. When I was angry at Him, I also began to question what I knew was truth, and it became frightening.

July 2022 will mark two years since my world was turned upside-down and my life was changed forever. I have since found a new church that is much smaller than the one where my mom and I were members, and they have embraced me as one of their family. I have finished and published a children's book that I had started before my mom passed away. I just wish that she was here to see it.

I am learning—though I still cry out over missing my mom and sometimes find myself still wanting to tell her things, like about the exciting events that have happened in my life—to lean on God once again. I think my life and my faith have gone deeper through this journey. It's a faith that is not based on certainty but rather, on a trust in God even though I don't understand.

Even when it seems dark, even when it feels like you are all alone and all you want to do is curl up in the fetal position and cry, it's okay. Just do it. Grief will come and go, kind of like waves from the ocean. Remember, the pain will probably never go away completely, but it does get easier to get through with each passing week, month, and year.

My Grief Journey: Les Beimers

A Century on Earth

When you live to be one hundred years old, many assume that much loss and heartache have been a part of your life. Most of that grief typically takes place later in life, but I knew grief as a child, and I've experienced grief repeatedly throughout my long life. I was blessed to be raised in a faithful household, and faith was (and is) an integral part of my everyday life.

I was one of nine children, and two of my brothers were diagnosed with multiple sclerosis. Back in the early 1920s, there were no medications or physical therapy services available for those who suffered from this disease. I have memories of carrying both of my brothers everywhere because they didn't have wheelchairs. My older brother suffered from age seventeen to age twenty-nine before he succumbed to the disease. My younger brother lived to the age of fifty-nine, as more therapies emerged.

While death was a mystery to me at a young age, and I missed my older brother, I was relieved for him. I had witnessed his journey of helplessness and pain. In truth, it was more difficult watching my parents as they grieved deeply for their sons. I've outlived my entire family, but I never got used to saying goodbye to each of my parents and every sibling. No one ever "gets used to" death.

I was married to my wife, Nellie, for twenty-five years. We had three beautiful daughters, Carol, Jan, and Judy. Nellie suffered from mental and physical illnesses that left me caring for our daughters for most of their childhood. Bath time was a highlight in the evenings, and I quickly learned how to braid hair and what pigtails were. Nellie spent a lot of time in Pine Rest, a nursing facility, and was absent from the home. She died after an epileptic seizure.

I was blessed to meet and marry Evie in 1966 when my daughters were adults. I found myself starting over, however, because Evie had two young children.

My daughters suffered the effects of not having a mother present in their lives because their mother was not strong enough to help raise them. Our youngest, Judy, struggled with alcoholism, which ultimately caused her death when she was in her forties. She was my first child loss. While her death wasn't a surprise, I experienced complicated grief.

"Could I have done anything differently?" This question plagued my thoughts.

Both feelings of guilt and relief were present. Evie and I had received countless calls in the middle of the night, times when Judy had gotten into predicaments or placed herself in danger. I felt that, with Judy's death, she could be at peace in the Lord, away from the demons that had destroyed her and our family over and over. There was no obituary, no visitation, no funeral. Judy's disjointed family wished for no services or public notifications.

Our oldest daughter, Carol, was diagnosed with Crohn's disease in her thirties and suffered for over seventeen years. She and her lovely family lived in Indiana. We worried about her every day. Though we'd received many calls over the years about her hospitalizations, one day, when her husband called us—on April 2, 2015—it was different. He let us know that she was worse than ever before. She wanted to talk with us but was so ill that she couldn't engage in a conversation. Later that evening, we received the call that no parent wants to receive. Carol had passed away. It was heartbreaking to lose another daughter. We truly believe Carol's daughters and son began grieving well before her death, having witnessed their mother experience the pain and suffering over time. We traveled to Indiana for Carol's service, and we hurt deeply as we watched her children in such pain. We are fortunate to keep in close touch with Carol's family even today.

Our middle daughter, Jan, was very attentive and loving before and after the death of her sisters. Her husband and two children were close to us, and we enjoyed many happy times together. Jan was a talented upholsterer and shared her talent by teaching others the craft. Jan and Gene purchased a second home in Florida with great anticipation of retiring there and enjoying many moments with family.

That plan was shattered when Jan began experiencing pain while at their home in Florida. She visited a doctor and found out that she had stage 4 ovarian cancer. They quickly returned to Michigan to seek care. After three months of chemo treatments, Jan's health continued to deteriorate, and she succumbed to this awful disease in 2017.

How can this be happening again? I thought.

I would never have thought I would live this long life . . . and outlive all of my children. At times, this reality still overwhelms me. But I am so grateful that God brought Evie to me because I can't imagine walking this journey of losing my three daughters without her love, support, and our faith. Marrying her and joining her two young children, David and Jill, blessed my life—then and now—as I have no more biological children on earth. David and Jill and their families fill my life with much love and joy.

Faith. In my one hundred years on this earth, our Lord and Savior has walked beside me every step of the way. With each passing decade and the loss of so many in my life, whom I loved dearly, God has provided comfort, peace, and strength that I could never have mustered up by myself. I couldn't do life without the Lord.

When struggles and tests come your way, if you are a believer and you trust in the Lord, you will find the strength to go on and experience a joy to share with others. Even through the pain, the Lord opens many doors to joy. Until my dying day, I will always look for His open doors.

My Grief Journey: Danielle Josephine Dewitt

My Special Aunt and Godmother

My aunt Tudi was a daughter, wife, mother, and friend. When I was born, my parents chose her to be my godmother, and I do not remember a time when I didn't feel a special bond with her. There is a picture of her and me taken on my first Easter. She was holding me up as I was learning to walk, which is a perfect metaphor for how I thought of her. Aunt Tudi was a source of joy, encouragement, and the person I could be at my most vulnerable.

I find it surprising how crystal clear the details of her last month on this earth still are. The loss of my aunt, godmother, and friend was sudden; and it is only recently that I have been able to truly process the magnitude of losing her. She was forty-four years old. Come to think of it, she was the same age I am as I write this.

In the early hours of February 8, 2001, my mom received a call from my uncle; aunt Tudi had fallen out of bed and her heart had stopped. I awoke to my mom telling me that I needed to go with her so I could be with my cousins. It was cold and dark—the kind of cold that makes your teeth chatter. I can still picture the flashing lights of the ambulance as we drove up and the paramedic telling my mom to follow them to the hospital right away. I ran into the house and my uncle said, "It's bad, Danielle."

They headed to the emergency room, and I sat in the sun-room, praying, while her three children—ages nine, eleven, and thirteen—slept peacefully. There was a moment when I realized they would be waking up soon, and I would have to "put on my game face." If I remember correctly, her youngest, Alissa, was the first to wake up and find me sitting in the sunroom. At that moment in time, we had no idea what was happening, other than her mom was at the hospital. I took a deep breath and did my best to remain calm. It was not the time to speculate, even though my mind was flirting with very dark places. Joel, Daniel, Alissa, and I began the morning routine but eventually decided it was a good day to stay home.

Later that day, I sat in the waiting room at the hospital, antic-ipating my turn to see her. It all felt so surreal. The tubes, wires, and monitors that beeped as they measured her vital signs . . . there was a numbness that took over, and I went into autopilot, which would last for a while. Over the next few weeks, we prayed for a miracle. This would prove to be a time filled with insur-mountable challenges to our faith. This was the first time I had ever felt angry with God.

What did not help were the words, "This is all part of God's plan," or the many iterations of this particular platitude that I heard throughout these days and the following weeks. Then, in what left me with the biggest questions of all, our family heard what we had been praying never to hear; there would be no miracle. Aunt Tudi was not going to wake up.

She was moved to Breton Manor, a nursing home with a hospice wing. This move added another layer to my sadness and confusion—the feeling that we were giving up. It was time to face what would be the biggest challenge to my faith; it was time to say goodbye to this incredible human whom we all loved and adored.

When I visited her new space, the first thing I noticed was how peaceful Aunt Tudi looked. There were no more beeping machines, just the sound of her oxygen and the soft music that was playing for her. One positive of her new environment was that hospice would allow us to come and go as we pleased and stay for however long we wanted, which was a welcome change.

While all of this was happening, I was in school and had a full-time job. I was thankful to my employer and my teammates who supported me throughout these days, which gave me some flexibility. It would have been easy to just stop going to school, but I knew that Aunt Tudi would never have wanted that. Education was very important to her.

One of the cruel ironies of this time in my life was that the one person I was used to talking to and leaning on when life seemed like it'd become too much was Aunt Tudi. As much as they reminded us that she could hear us, speaking out loud to her seemed difficult. So I began using writing as a coping mechanism and wrote her letters. In the beginning, these letters were my way of being able to tell her all of the things I wanted to when she woke up. As time moved forward, they were an outlet, a way to express my feelings in the only way that made sense. Today, these letters remain in my "Aunt Tudi Box" along with the cards she had given me over the years.

Aunt Tudi was in hospice care for ten days. I am so grateful for the compassionate individuals who watched over her and cared for her during those ten days. They not only looked out for her but were incredibly supportive of my uncle, the kids, and our entire family.

On March 8, 2001, unbeknownst to me, I made what would be my last solo visit to spend time with her. I had brought something special—my laptop and a Barbra Streisand concert DVD. Aunt Tudi and I had dreamed of getting to see her perform one day. This would be as close as we'd ever get, and I like to think she could hear it all.

Two days later, on March 10, 2001, the hospice team told us the end was near, and almost all of our family members made their way there. As day turned to night, the decision was made for me to bring her children home. We talked on the way home about watching a movie and after we had been at the house for about twenty minutes, the phone rang. My mom shared that Aunt Tudi had taken her last breath and asked me to drive the kids back.

We drove back in silence, and somehow, I managed to drive them all there without one tear. As we walked toward her room and the kids went in, I could do nothing except allow myself to cry—the kind of "ugly cry" where you aren't quite sure how to make it stop. That was the beginning of the grieving process.

I have found ways to honor her memory. Occasionally, I will write her a letter, and it goes into my "Aunt Tudi box." And every March 8, I have an "Aunt Tudi Day," when I try to find ways to celebrate her through acts of service; I take a little time to read through the letters, and, of course, watch the Barbra Streisand concert.

It's been twenty-one years since she left us, and over these two decades, I've spent a lot of time thinking about her and working through my grief, layer by layer. There is a quote I read recently from author Elizabeth Gilbert that I want to share with others who are in their grieving process.

> *Grief is a force of energy that cannot be controlled or predicted. It comes and goes on its own schedule. Grief does not obey your plan or your wishes. Grief will do whatever it wants to you, whenever it wants to. In that way, Grief has a lot in common with Love.*

I miss her so much, and I'm grateful she was a part of my life.

My Grief Journey: Steve Kelly

Tormented by Grief

It was a foggy, rainy evening, March 9, 1979, not far outside of Upper Heyford Air Force Base in England. My best friend, John Gerard, and I hitched a ride to his parent's house for a sleepover. He was thirteen; I was fourteen. John was popular, extroverted, and a confident leader, even at that age. Since I was a painfully shy introvert and follower, it wasn't even a thought that I'd take the back seat, putting John in the front seat next to the adult. As our conversation wound down, we relaxed into the short drive and kept to our thoughts, maybe even nodding off. I remember looking up through the wet windshield in the limited light of dusk at a confusing sight. I don't remember being shocked or scared, just baffled to see the car's lights falling on a wall of hay.

Friendships between military brats can develop quickly and intensely. When you start from scratch every couple of years, there is comfort in kindred spirits, and John and I were very close, though we had only known each other for a relatively short time. You see, my parents divorced when I was very young. My relationship with my father eventually disintegrated into a series of heartbreaking disappointments—for my sister and me—as he fought his demons of depression and alcohol abuse. When my mother found love again, it was with an old classmate from Ludington, then serving in the Air Force. We blended our families and headed out, first to the Upper Peninsula at K.I. Sawyer, where our step-siblings stripped off, and next to RAF Croughton where just my sister and I made the trip. That move was particularly devastating because I then lost the important relationship with the man who had taken my troubled father's place—my grandfather, Bob. Long-distance communication was far from what it is now and since my stepfather and I were on different wavelengths, I was filling in some of my developmental gaps myself. At fourteen, I was anxious, lonely, and troubled.

I don't remember how long I pondered the wall of hay, but next came an explosion of sound and the violent compaction as our vehicle crashed underneath a semi-truck overloaded with hay bales at what was later determined to be about fifty-five miles per hour. Our vehicle didn't have time to break, and the car was wedged in at the door handles. I still remember some distinctive sounds (and the lack thereof) that came immediately following the accident. Fluid dripped but otherwise, silence. Then a noise came from just above me that has haunted me for forty-three years: my friend John's labored last breath.

The new silence was deafening to my soul.

As our driver came to consciousness with moans, it became obvious to us that the dripping liquid was fuel, and the terror of waiting for the vehicle to catch on fire took the place of my shock and despair. We were trapped in the wreckage and began to scream. I can't describe the feeling as our panicked cries became a chorus. Eventually, the driver of the truck was able to fish his hand into the wreckage and touch my head. It was as if God himself was telling me it would be okay. Once the first responders arrived, it took two hours to cut me out of the twisted metal, the roof peeled from the back end of the car. Throughout most of that time, I could see the wind catch the blond hair of my lifeless friend.

We didn't know much about treating PTSD, depression, and anxiety—or even survivor's guilt—in those days. Especially not on a small Air Force base in England. My parents did the best they could by protecting me and insisting we just carry on.

The day after the accident, I remember telling my mother that I wanted to go to church.

Although in shock, God had gotten my attention, and I had nowhere else to turn. God was to use this event as a springboard for our deepening relationship. As it turns out, the devil would also count on this event as a central theme to torment me too. We went to church as a family and rarely missed a Sunday. It was what laid the foundational base for my lifelong faith journey.

A year later, after spending most of my life as a "Christmas and Easter Christian," I accepted Jesus Christ as my personal Lord and Savior.

God almost singularly sustained me during those years. I am forever grateful for that little base church with its rotating ministers. I never talked to the Gerard family again. John had a younger sister, Tina, and my mom and John's dad have exchanged Christmas cards since, a bond made in tragedy. My mom keeps her Christmas cards in a basket, and I read them every year. And continued to get pangs of guilt.

Though I grew up and moved past this traumatic chapter in my life, the patch that I placed over this childhood injury would eventually come loose. Although I had a successful radio career, a happy marriage, and two beautiful children, addiction would enter my life. Medicating with alcohol for anxiety and depression culminated in a deadly diagnosis of liver disease. Unresolved childhood trauma only exacerbated my mental challenges.

After admitting my powerlessness to my Savior, real healing occurred through intense therapy and Alcoholics Anonymous (AA). I have now been sober for eight years and have reversed my liver damage. I cannot explain how liberating it is not to be controlled by addiction.

My parents didn't get a Christmas card from the Gerards last year but did get a letter revealing that my friend John's mother had passed. I mentioned earlier that every year, I picked through my parents' cards to find the Gerards' card and read about my long-lost friend's family—his sister Tina, Andre, and Ingrid. Every year, in my guilt and unworthiness, I wished that I could apologize for being the one that lived.

While talking to my wife about what I should do next, she suggested I find them and reach out. It didn't take long to find Tina on social media, and I wrote an awkward message describing who I was, said a prayer, and hit send. Then, in our quiet living room, I got her response,

Holy cow, you found the right Tina!

She was with her dad. It had been almost forty-one years. Their grace made it seem as if the weight of a truck was taken off my shoulders.

If any of this story resonates with you, I invite you to admit your powerlessness and exhaust every resource to make yourself whole again. There is help; there is hope; you are not alone, and it's never too late. God bless you.

My Grief Journey: Nancy Poland

The Long Goodbye

I knew about grief, having lost family members and a few friends. The loss of a job, a relationship, and even a move across the country by a family member caused me to grieve. I knew someday my parents would die, and I would grieve. It is part of life, I reasoned, something we learn to live with.

What I was not prepared for was the long grieving process that started when my dad was diagnosed with dementia. They call dementia "the long goodbye," and for six years, we bounced between hope, distress, and sorrow. For a long time, I did not recognize grief. Instead, it was as though night was slowly descending on us, squeezing out the last rays of light.

Dementia brings the loss of plans and dreams. I remember the time my dad's nephew sent him a computer, a big chunky desktop machine. Dad was determined to master this new world. However, try as he might, he could not remember how to log in from one day to the next. Finally, he agreed to get rid of it, sadly saying, "There goes another lost dream."

More of his dreams died, and a little bit of me died with each of his losses. We decided to move our parents out of their house where they had lived for fifty years—my dad's pride and joy. He had designed an extra room for their home office, made special built-in cupboards for storage, and put a spare bathroom in the basement. (As the father of four daughters, that bathroom was needed!) By the time my parents moved out of the house into a one-level townhome, Dad could not remember how to assemble a flashlight due to his dementia. It was a hot July day when we loaded up their household goods, sadness gripping our hearts.

Driving became a major issue. Picture a late '70s model cargo van, smaller than a regular-sized van. Now, envision a series of dents and dings on the brown and beige vehicle; this was what our dad drove. The damage to the van became more frequent as time went on. When questioned about it, Dad would report, "I was turning right, and this woman wasn't looking. She plowed right into me!" I often wondered why he did not get stopped by the police . . . until he shared a ticket with me. "That cop is trying to ruin my life!" I looked at the ticket, and the police officer had written down five other times Dad had been stopped in the last year but not ticketed. We tried to convince Dad to quit driving, to no avail. Finally, he was ordered to retake the driving test. While he passed that time, it wasn't long until he was stopped again by the local police and ordered to take an assessment. We took him to the VA clinic where he had been receiving care; they tested his reactions and abilities. At the end of the appointment, they informed him he could no longer drive. While this was the outcome our family had hoped for, it gave me no joy on the quiet, sobering ride home. Little by little, everything we knew about our dad was slipping away into a shell of the hard-working, storytelling guy everyone loved.

Then, suddenly, I understood the true meaning of grief. My mom had been previously diagnosed with kidney cancer. After removing one kidney, she had three good years where she appeared to have overcome the cancer. But then, back it came with a vengeance—a few cells had escaped, and the cancer had spread to her lungs. After a three-week hospital stay and five days of home hospice, my mom passed away. I knew she was home in Heaven, but the sorrow of her passing was overwhelming. I grieved, and grief was my master for a time.

Then, the question came, *what do we do about Dad?* He clearly could not live alone, so we moved him into a senior apartment building with extra services, such as meals, and oversite by the nursing staff. However, as time progressed, Dad became less able to function. A story and joke teller all his life, Dad's biggest joy was swapping tales with people. At first, he made friends in the apartment building and attended group activities, but within a year, he could barely put a sentence together. Using hesitation and broken speech, he told us, "The other guys can tell stories. I can't now."

After they found him on the floor, unable to get up, we had to make a change. If I had any doubt about grief, it now hit me from all sides. How could my strong, smart, competent father, a World War II veteran, business owner, and caretaker of his wife and four daughters become so debilitated? It wasn't just his memory; it was his ability to process information, called "executive functioning," and his gait and movements were affected. We had to place him in a nursing home because he needed so much care.

I remember leaving the nursing home one night, with tears streaming down my face. I wondered, *Why doesn't someone stop me? Why don't they ask me if I'm okay?* Perhaps they were just used to people outwardly grieving, and they had too many tasks caring for patients to worry about one woman's pain.

My tears were not isolated and, recognizing my frequent crying and depression were unmanageable, I sought medical care. I was placed on anti-depressants and sought other help. We then had to move Dad from the nursing home to more advanced memory care. Soon, he could not walk or talk, becoming completely incapacitated. I grieved, I prayed God would take him home. Finally, one night, I received the call. Dad had died peacefully during the night. I had grieved so much over the last six years that there were no tears left for his funeral. I had a certain peace because finally, his suffering was over.

This is not to say I have not grieved for both of my parents since they died. After his death, I pondered writing our story, but it took me six years to process Dad's illness and death in my mind before I could start writing. Finally, I published a book about my dad's Lewy Body dementia called *Dancing With Lewy: A Father-Daughter Dance Before and After Lewy Body Dementia Came to Live With Us.* I hope this book will help others struggling with the care of their loved ones.

I am a better person having cared for my parents through their final years on this earth. It has made me more tolerant and aware of people with disabilities. Caring for my dad during the haze of dementia brought us closer than we had ever been, and I learned much about his life and his heart.

Grief taught me the meaning of true love. None of us want to go through grief, and sometimes, we do not recognize this form of sorrow when it starts to wrap itself around our hearts. We often wonder, *What is the meaning of suffering?* I'm not a theologian, but this I know: sorrow and grief are part of this journey in our broken world. God made us to be eternal, and when people depart this earth, grief is the path of brokenness we must walk. But this I also know: I will see my parents again when we are united in Heaven at the feet of Jesus, and this gives me great hope.

My Grief Journey: Vonnie Woodrick

> ### *Love Never Dies. It Grows Stronger*

The most difficult part of my after-loss journey is watching my kids grow up without their dad. How do you tell a five-year-old that their dad died by suicide?

I thought suicide was something a crazy person did. My husband wasn't crazy. He was kind, loving, gentle, and fun. He made me laugh; he made our kids laugh, yet he lived with anxiety that could turn into debilitating depression.

I didn't know depression could kill. I didn't know because we don't talk about it like that. Depression is an illness, one that takes almost one million of our friends, family members, neighbors, and co-workers worldwide each year. But we continue to act surprised when it happens.

My husband, Rob, didn't choose depression, nor did the three generations before him. Yet this effect of depression is considered a choice. Do people living with other illnesses choose their illness? Do they choose to die when their organs, blood, or bones fail them?

I began to ask questions, which I notice many don't ask. "Why is the brain the only organ in our body that is judged when it fails or becomes weak? Why do we talk more about the "act" rather than the illness? Why do we judge mental and brain illness yet grieve suicide?"

I am still in search of answers. I found myself very alone after my loss. Most didn't understand and offered advice though they had never experienced this type of devastating loss.

Many would say to me, "Get through the first year; the first year is always the hardest." I plowed my way through the first year, anticipating the grief-free pot of gold at the end of the rainbow, but it wasn't there. The pot of gold was empty.

That empty feeling lingered throughout my journey, not just through the first year but through the second, the third, and now the eighteenth. The anticipation of something magical happening once I "got through the first year" made the second more difficult than the first.

Rather than hiding behind my husband's death, I started talking about it. I wanted to talk about how my husband lived, not how he died. He was so much more than his illness, yet so many were focused on his death. Most didn't know what to say or how to include the kids or me. Our "couple friends" disappeared. I would get the occasional, "Mike is out of town. Want to meet for dinner?" Those times of feeling left out—or being included and then not wanting to go—made for an emotional roller coaster ride.

I began changing the way I talked about suicide because it was dark and scary and unknown to me. I stopped lying. Rather than telling others that he died in a more acceptable way—like a car accident, cancer, or heart attack—I began telling the truth.

My husband died from depression.

Many look at me strangely because they only understand to say he "committed suicide," "completed," or even "killed" himself. Those comments make me cringe and my stomach sink to the depths.

Following a suicide loss is the most dreaded, most asked question: "How did he do it?"

Really? I had just experienced the most devastating, difficult, and painful loss imaginable, and you are asking me, "How?" It brings me back to that moment, the moment that has become a nightmarish vision every time I close my eyes. The moment that keeps me from opening any closed white door. The moment my life changed.

The questions forced me to suffer from self-proclaimed, "turtle syndrome." I would head out to the reality of having to grocery shop or pick up one of the kids at a school function. Next, I would get the "look of shock" from people not knowing what to do or say to someone whose husband just killed himself, or I would hear the whispers in the same vain as the looks I would receive. That was hard.

I forced myself back into my turtle shell. I would slowly peak out and venture out, praying I would not run into someone I knew because the questions, the whispers, and the pointing were too much for my broken heart to handle.

I was tired of feeling alone in a crowded room. I was hurt by those who were defining my husband by how he died rather than how he lived. My kids needed peace. My kids needed understanding.

My love for my children allowed me to see something that many have a difficult time seeing after any type of loss or the grief they live with: It's not time that heals, but rather, time just goes away. It is love that heals, and love can stay a long time.

We created the non-profit called i understand love heals[10] because we understand something that many won't ever deal with, admit to, or even seek help for. *Mental illness.*

Learning as much as I could while supporting my children after four generations of suicide loss, I had more questions. Why isn't the genetic component talked about? Why do we cover up and swipe mental illness under the rug? Why don't we call it "brain illness?" Isn't it our brains that are in pain or not functioning properly?

The CDC (Centers for Disease Control) states that over 54 percent of those who die by suicide do *not* have a diagnosed mental health illness. Yet 90 percent of those who die are living with depression. Does that make sense?

This means that more than half of those who die by suicide are experiencing some form of pain, which is leading them to depression. Pain is something we all live with at some point in our lives. Couldn't we all be at risk if it is pain that brings on undiagnosed depression?

Depression is an illness. It is treatable. It is preventable. Most other illnesses that our bodies can face are just like depression—treatable and preventable, and some of these illnesses can be considered terminal. We now know that even the flu can be terminal. Then why can't our brains suffer from a terminal illness?

My husband had an illness; I didn't know that depression had this deadly effect. Once I did, I was able to take some of the guilt away from the suicide loss because I knew this: he didn't choose his illness; therefore, how could he choose his death?

Didn't he just want his pain to end?

My husband left me the gift of passion. It took me a while to feel this gift, but once I did, it ran deep. It's a bittersweet truth to know I had to lose Rob to find it. It's a passion to remove the stigma and change the views and narratives surrounding the topic of depression and suicide, freeing those who are struggling to seek help, removing the guilt and dampening the shame of those who have lost, and understanding that "love never dies; it grows stronger."

My Grief Journey: Jeff Elhart

| **The Loss of My Brother** |

I found Wayne dead on March 27, 2015. My brother had suffered from depression for a relatively short time before he took his life. He had been my partner for thirty-two years in the family business. He had also been my best friend. I could hardly get past the shock of his death. Once I did, I was plagued with an unanswered question: *Why?*

Survivors of suicide always feel anger or guilt—sometimes both. I wasn't angry at my brother or God. But I was seriously struggling with guilt. I kept questioning myself. *Why didn't I help him? How did I not notice what was going on? What could I have done to prevent it?* Incessantly, relentlessly, these questions kept nagging at me. I felt some solace in knowing I had sensed something was going on in his last months. I had gotten him to his primary care physician and helped him discover faith in God. But that wasn't enough. Something was missing, and it kept me awake at night.

Releasing my guilt was important to my mental health. Thanks to a message I heard in a movie, one that I had soaked in two months after my brother's death, I am free of the majority of my guilt. What was that message? It came in the form of a story where a high school boy loses his father to depression by suicide. He, like me, struggles with the two unique emotions associated with a death by suicide: anger and guilt. In his case, he struggles most with anger. In his journey to find the "why" his father took his life, the boy, named Jackson, discovers a sign from his father in the form of a note representing his struggle in life. Through a series of events, Jackson continues to struggle with his quest to find out why his father took his life—so much so that he finds himself about to jump off the same bridge his father did. He is saved by his counselor, but while contemplating jumping, Jackson realizes his father had died of a mental illness. There was not anything Jackson did. The story ends when Jackson takes the reminders of his anger and burns them in his backyard. The next day, he takes the ashes of the reminders of his anger and spreads them around the base of a new tree that he and his mother and sister plant in memory of his father.

This movie gave me the idea that I needed to rid myself of the reminders of the guilt associated with my brother's death. I decided that I would do what Jackson did. In my case, I journaled every moment that I wish I would have done something about helping my brother before he died. Those six pages, filled with eleven specific situations, I buried in an urn containing Wayne's cremains. At that moment, I felt the weight leave my shoulders as if God was lifting me off of the ground. Immediately, I felt the Holy Spirit free me of my guilt.

Having been blessed with freedom from my guilt, I still knew that while I had missed an opportunity with Wayne, other people like him needed help. What if there was a tool that could equip people to identify mental illness in others and then help them get the help they need? I had noticed signs of Wayne's depression, but I honestly had not known what to do. What if there was a way for people to know?

Even though it was too late to save Wayne, I could honor a request he left in his suicide note, which we did not discover until months after his death. "God, please use me to help others," he wrote. This became my mission.

I dove into research. I consumed all kinds of books and resources about depression and suicide. I learned a lot, but nothing struck me as something I could use to equip everyday people in a meaningful way. Then I met Christy Buck, executive director of The Mental Health Foundation of West Michigan[11]. That organization had developed a tool called be nice., which forms an acrostic with the word nice. It is easy to learn and easy to teach. It came as a specific answer to one of the biggest prayers of my life.

Be nice. has changed my life and the lives of many others. As of this writing, over 150,000 K–12 students and 250,000 adults have experienced the impact of this life-saving tool. The program has enlisted a donor-advised fund of the Community Foundation of the Holland/Zeeland Area to provide matching funds to school districts in four Michigan counties that commit to the Mental Health Foundation of West Michigan be nice. program on mental illness and suicide prevention education. Furthermore, the Elhart family has teamed with two other West Michigan families—the Braganini family from Kalamazoo and the Lubbers family from Grand Rapids—to initiate similar funds to reach students in four additional Michigan counties. The funds are also involved in supporting be nice. in police departments, businesses, schools, veteran associations, and more. Experts at Grand Valley State University have conducted a study that affirms its effectiveness. It is well on its way to changing the way people think about and respond to mental illness, depression, and potential suicide.

One out of every four people in the world will suffer from some level of depression or mental illness this year. More than two-thirds of those people will not seek or receive professional treatment. Those who do not suffer from depression don't understand how it feels or the agony it causes each day it is left untreated. It is a painful but too often unaddressed illness for those who have it; it's an invisible one for those who don't.

That's where you come in. I didn't know how to help Wayne, but you have the opportunity to make it visible—to arm yourself with the tools that can help you and others deal with this problem. What are you going to do with that opportunity? How are you going to equip yourself to help your loved ones, your friends, your co-workers, your associates, and your acquaintances in your community or at your church?

You can start right now. After hearing the message of be nice., you will be armed with the knowledge to help others improve and even save their lives. Mental illness is treatable, and suicide is preventable. And you are part of the solution. You can help. All you have to do is *be nice.*

My Grief Journey: Janet V. Grillo

Being YOU Matters

Everyone has a story, but many do not feel their story is worth telling. God often chooses to use us to help others by recovering from our tragedies. Although my front story is different from everyone else's, our backstories are the same.

We have all fallen to our knees and prayed to God for help. We have all had anxiety attacks, and many of us have had out-of-body experiences where we wondered if we could make it through the next day, let alone the next hour.

My husband died tragically on December 13, 2001. To this day, I do not know if his death was a suicide, assisted suicide, suggested suicide, or murder. After his death, I discovered that he lived a double life, engaging in numerous affairs, and was allegedly part of the Philadelphia mafia. I had a nervous breakdown, experienced anxiety attacks daily, entertained suicidal thoughts, and fell into a state of depression. I had so many questions. I wondered how I could make sense of it all.

Where was God, and why did He let this happen? What use was there in going on? Could I ever find joy and hope again? Did I have a purpose anymore, or had it gone to the grave with my husband?

After months of closing my bedroom door to the outside world, lying in the fetal position, I heard a voice from the television say, "Why are you lying there feeling sorry for yourself? You are the only one responsible for your happiness."

The voice was Joyce Meyer's. Joyce is an American Charismatic Christian, author, and speaker. Her father and other relatives sexually assaulted her throughout her childhood. She turned to God for help. With God's help, she turned ashes into beauty and made a difference in many lives. Shortly after hearing Joyce Meyer's message from God, I stumbled across an infomercial by Tony Robbins. Tony was selling his Personal Power II—The Driving Force program, a thirty-day program designed to empower people to take back control of their lives and make the changes that would transform their lives from ordinary to extraordinary.

I had trouble committing to anything. However, I ordered the course and prayed that I could commit to improving the quality of my life for at least thirty days. Although I was afraid to venture outside the four walls of my bedroom, I mustered up the courage to take daily walks. Tony shared how he had hit rock bottom, living in his car, when a dream entered his heart. He knew the only way to succeed was to read every book he could on self-improvement and apply what he learned. He discovered that success came by educating himself and then helping others to succeed by assisting them in understanding that their powers lie within themselves. When the tapes arrived, I set baby-step goals to listen to one lesson a day and do my best to apply what I had learned. Each session ended with a homework assignment to write in a journal by answering questions supplied in the program.

Day 1's session was titled "The Key to Personal Power," and that day's assignment posed two questions. "What two decisions have I been putting off, which, if I make now, will change my life?" I thought for a moment then wrote, *Stop feeling sorry for myself. Stop thinking about the circumstances around my husband's death and move on.* I moved to the second question: "What three different things can I do that will be consistent with my two decisions?" Again, I thought and then wrote: *(1) Start writing in a journal to release my thoughts, anger, and disappointments. (2) Start eating nutritiously and take daily walks. (3) Start each day by reading positive quotations and affirmations.*

My favorite quote is by Sandra Carey. "Never mistake knowledge for wisdom. One helps you make a living; the other helps you make a life." Sitting back, I put down my pen and thanked God again for how He had led me to these messages from Joyce Meyer and Tony Robbins. Once again, I cried out for help, and God answered my prayers. But, thinking about these two people and their influence made me wonder, *Has God been trying to talk to me on other occasions through other ordinary people, but I did not recognize His help? Could my healing have started sooner, but I was too stubborn to open my eyes to see or my ears to hear?*

Ever since I was a child, people have made fun of me, accusing me of being a dreamer. Despite their criticism, I continued to have big dreams, though I kept them primarily to myself. But God seemed to be saying to my heart that He saw more in me than I had ever seen in myself. I heard God say that my dreams weren't nearly as big as the dreams He had for me . . . for all of us.

It's incredible how God draws upon ordinary people in our lives to plant seeds of quests, encouragement, love, and more. He planted a seed in me to write my book, *God Promised Me Wings to Fly: Life for Survivors After Suicide.* Although the book's subtitle is Life for Survivors After Suicide, it is an excellent read for anyone who has suffered a tragedy.

I was in Mr. Fox's remedial reading class in the seventh grade. I thought plenty of people were more qualified than me to write the book. But God works differently from how we view things. When God expands our territory, it is not about our skill; it's about God's will. I created a plan to be the best person and live my best life in time. I knew becoming the best person wasn't just for my healing; it was to reach beyond myself to help others. I had to gain much wisdom and go through much pain to heal appropriately before allowing myself to help others get through their grief. It would be disingenuous to try to help others if I was not in a healthy place.

We are all children of God, no matter our age. Unfortunately, many children have lost their way. There is no promise of tomorrow in the Bible. We must treat each day as a gift from God and cherish every moment.

When my granddaughter, Mackenzie, was four years old, she asked, "Mom-Mom, do you know that I have special powers?" *I wish that I was nocturnal because then I could see in the dark; I would think that seeing in the dark would be part of her special powers. However, to a four-year-old, it made perfect sense.*

"No, I did not know that you had special powers," I said, looking most impressed. "Where can I get some?"

"All you have to do is ask God, and He will give them to you," she said, smilingly brightly.

Today, Mackenzie is twenty years old. At the age of four, she knew that she had special powers. She also had a thirst for a clearer vision to see in the dark.

As we get closer to God, we will begin to remove ourselves from the darkness. We will discover that God's light and powers are within all of us. It is our job to find out what is already there. I am amazed that such wisdom came from a four-year-old.

When all of God's children understand that we are not alone and discover that we are the only ones who can embrace our special powers—special healing powers that do not disappear when tragedy and pain enter our lives—we will be changed, healed, and empowered. And in turn, we will use those special healing powers to make a difference in the lives of others.

God promised me wings to fly. He promised you wings to fly as well. There is hope in surviving a tragedy . . . and not just surviving, but truly thriving and making the world a better place, not despite the tragedy, but because of it.

My Grief Journey: David Morris, Phd

Grief Comes in Many Forms

In the early summer before eighth grade, my parents let my two sisters and I know that we were moving across the country so my dad could take a new job. We were living in 1970s Southern California, wrapped in the familiar world of family, friends, and

Taco Bells, the only life I knew to that point. After the news had sunk in, I remember saying through tears, "Will I ever see Rob?" As it turns out, I wouldn't see my best friend much at all as life continued. My family and I were off to Northern Virginia, facing tremendous change, and there was no small amount of loneliness for this twelve-year-old boy.

Discovering that friendships are not always something you can keep immediately present in your everyday life was one of my first meaningful experiences with loss and grief. It's not the same thing for a preteen boy as losing a parent or sibling or friend to death, but what I have come to learn, even though it goes against our everyday hopes and dreams, is that loss and grief are an omnipresent part of living.

I made it a point to study the topic of loss as I went from being a psychology major in college to a doctoral program where I focused specifically on the psychology of faith loss. There, I fully realized how losing one's religion is not just about no longer believing in certain things; it also means losing so many of the relationships and traditions that surrounded those beliefs. It is a loss of identity, a communal past, which is a tricky kind of loss.

As life has gone on, I have experienced a lot of other losses, especially now that I am well into middle age. I am fortunate that my parents are still alive, but their parents are long gone, especially my dad's father who died of pancreatic cancer when my dad was just an infant. Now, there's an imprint of loss that doesn't easily go away. Aunts and uncles are now gone. Then there are other losses, more traumatic ones, like a struggling cousin who died by suicide, another cousin from a hidden heart anomaly, and a phenomenally successful co-worker, also shockingly by suicide.

When I think philosophically about it now, I realize that loss comprises many things, one being the loss of what might have been or what was to come.

One of the hardest losses I have ever faced came when I was fired from a job as a vice president and publisher at a big-time publishing company. I had moved my family from the East Coast to the Midwest—which was significant given my past—for an opportunity to gain experience professionally and establish us financially. I was a good leader in my role at this new job, and our team was consistently thriving in a rapidly changing marketplace. But nothing is perfect, and the management took the route of thinking they needed a leadership change. I'll leave out the details but for this one thing, which may seem small. When the pivotal meeting informing me I was no longer employed took place, my supervisor didn't look me in the eye. It was not because of the awkward video call; in an impersonal and detached manner, he just never looked directly at me while he read a script. It was chilling; though, at the time, I almost felt sorry for him because it also seemed immature for someone in a role of such authority.

In the weeks and months that followed, I paradoxically felt both waves of shock and relief, but also the sense that it did not have to be that way. I knew things were not ideal, but my team and I were working hard toward the ideal. The outcome could have been different, and there was still plenty to do together.

We feel loss more than we might realize. It is in the air we breathe. Each of these experiences with loss has been hard, wondering especially what could have been. But each loss has brought new horizons I never could have planned. I found a new job, though it's the big, hairy, audacious goal of starting my own publishing business. I may have moved a lot in life, but I have found new friends and have at least one close friend from just about every place I've lived.

A well-regarded child psychologist, Melanie Klein, once said that you must go backward in your loss to find that moment when you pined to know the object of your loss. You must rediscover that sense of hope and longing you had when you experienced mutual recognition and love in the relationship. I find that to be an affecting thought. It might seem to take an eternity, and those moments of pining may seem fewer and far between. But we all once felt whole, alive, and in love with the world around us. It's still there somewhere.

And if we're lucky, we keep in touch with those old friends. It's been a while, but I just got an email from Rob the other day.

My Grief Journey: Scott Winters

Man's Best Friends

We have all grieved over the loss of a loved one or friend. People understand when you are grieving the loss of a person, but what happens when you lose a furry family member?

I've found that *other* pet owners are quick to respond to your grief, but those that don't have pets don't understand how one can suffer so much grief over this type of loss. I can't tell you how many times I've heard, "Well, it was just a dog." Some reports say that symptoms of acute grief can last for a month or two, and on average, a person can grieve the loss of a pet for a full year. In my experience, it lasts much longer than that.

When I purchased my first home and advanced from "apartment living," one of the first things I wanted to do was to get a dog. I looked at several different breeds. I wanted a big dog, something over 100 pounds. I decided on an Old English Sheepdog. Everywhere I went, that little ball of fur named Barney was at my side. Barney was my best friend and companion. He was also a clown, making me laugh just about every day. Barney was like a very inquisitive child. No matter what I was doing, he was at my side watching as closely as he could. He was what I needed at that point in my life.

Unfortunately, I lost Barney to cancer when he was six years old. I was devastated. How could losing a pet hurt as much as, if not more than, losing a beloved family member or human friend? I felt a lot of guilt for my grief.

At the time of Barney's passing, I had another dog. Her name was Tally. The two of them spent a lot of time together as puppies. Eventually, Tally moved in with us. The two were great companions. After Barney's death, even Tally was not herself. We were both depressed. I put on my "happy face" around others, but deep down inside, my heart was shattered.

Shortly after Barney's passing, I was told about a rescued Newfoundland that needed a home. Her name was Molly. She was malnourished and hearing-impaired. I was asked to consider opening up my home to this poor girl. Of course, I said yes!

Molly Brown came to live with us. It was a good move for the three of us. I felt good knowing that I could offer a caring home to a dog who had lived a tough life. Both Tally and Molly lived to be about eleven years old, dying about a year apart.

Once again, I had to deal with the grieving process. I found it important to share my loss with others. The outpouring of kind words and prayers from fellow pet owners meant the world to me.

It took over a year before I felt I could open my home—and heart—to another dog. I was traveling out of state when something pulled me to stop by a pet store. I walked in to find several rescue dogs up for adoption. There was a medium-sized dog named Sadie who caught my eye. When she was let out of her crate, she immediately came over and pushed her nose between my arm and my body. She nuzzled as close to me as she could. It was evident; she wanted to go home with me. But it tore me apart because I just couldn't do it. I was hours from home. As hard as it was, I walked away, not looking back for fear I might lose my composure. I thought about that dog all week. The following weekend, I made a return four-hour trip to see if Sadie was still available. When I arrived back at the pet store, she was not there. I found the contact information for the shelter. I figured Sadie had found her forever home, and I was happy for her.

After returning home on Sunday evening, I checked out the shelter's website. There was Sadie, the featured dog! She was still available, but would they place her in a home so far away?

The next day, on Monday, I called the shelter. They emailed me an application, which I promptly filled out and returned. Within an hour, I was approved. The following week—for the third week in a row—I was back on the road to pick up Sadie, who looked like and therefore was re-named, Scooby.

A year later, I had a co-worker who had a litter of rat terrier puppies. There was one left. Repeatedly, my co-worker told me my home would be perfect for him. But he was a "small dog," and I was a "big dog" person. I went to look at him anyway. No surprise here, but I came home with that little guy, who was small in size but huge with personality and character. I chose the name that fit him best: Moose. The three of us spent years together. Not only were they my roommates, but also my travel companions. We traveled thousands of miles together over the years.

Many years later, Scooby suffered from doggie dementia and passed away at the age of fourteen. After she died, I knew I had to make Moose the focus of my attention. He had never been an "only dog," always having had Scooby by his side. Perhaps I went overboard spoiling Moose, but he meant so much to me. I could tell we were both grieving over the loss of Scooby.

One night, I arrived home to find the poor guy taking what seemed like his last breath. Immediately, we were on our way to the emergency animal hospital. My fear was he wasn't going to last long enough to get there. Moose ended up in intensive care for a few days. He had congestive heart failure. Moose needed the care of a cardiologist. It would be expensive, but I would find the money. I didn't care what the cost was. I had the resources to pay whatever was needed. (I can't imagine having to make a medical decision about my pet's life based on the money in my bank account. My heart breaks for people in that situation.) Moose's heart had several problems, including that his heart valves were not functioning properly. There was a medicine that could help, but it would eventually attack some of his other organs. He was given about a year to live.

I was fortunate to get about a year and a half before some of his other organs started to shut down. He was just months from turning sixteen years old when Moose died. Once again, I felt like my heart had been ripped from my body. This was the worst grief I have ever experienced in my life.

It has now been two years since Moose died, but I still find myself grieving over him. He was the little dog I didn't know I wanted, who'd become such a big part of my life. To help me through my ongoing grief, I started to dog sit for friends. A few times a month, I get to enjoy the company of a dog and then send them home after I have spoiled them for a few days.

It seems with every dog, the grief just gets worse. I'm not sure if that's because I'm getting older and more emotional over these types of things or what. The huge hole in my heart is still there, and it doesn't seem to be shrinking. Don't feel guilty, like I did, about the grief of a pet. It helps to search out other pet owners to talk to about the death of your furry friend. They understand what the pain feels like.

Will I ever get another dog? I'm not sure. It just doesn't feel right at the moment. I still miss Moose and all the others so much. From time to time, I swear I see him looking around the corner at me. I know he's still here in spirit, and he lives forever in my heart . . . until we all meet again.

DEVOTIONS

The Lord is my rock, my fortress and my deliverer;
my God is my rock, in whom I take refuge. He is my shield
and the horn of my salvation, my stronghold.

Psalm 18:2

In this section, we open God's Word to find the only true source of hope, comfort, and peace that comes during times of great loss.

These thirty devotions were prepared by members of the pastoral community in West Michigan who support individuals on the hospice journey and their loved ones.

Day One: Fr. Peter Vu

Scripture: Wisdom 4:13–14, NABRE

Having become perfect in a short while, he/she reached the fullness of a loving career; for his/her soul was pleasing to the Lord; therefore, the Lord sped him/her out of the midst of wickedness.

Devotional Reading: "Advice of a Counselor"

We find it difficult to say farewell to someone we know well and love dearly. We struggle a little more if that person seems to depart a bit too early from this world. We search high and low for an answer in our bewilderment. We wish that loved one would be around a little longer for us to show our affection or resolve an issue between him/her and us. As we try to make sense of our loved one's early departure, King Solomon, who was a wise counselor, tries to offer us his best explanation for our situation in the Scripture passage above. He believes that God calls our loved one home a bit early because God has found him/her worthy of a place in Heaven. God wants to preserve as many souls as possible from the wickedness of our world. That somber, wise explanation from King Solomon brings us much comfort and hope in this tough and confusing world. We can rest assured that God will take good care of our deceased loved ones until the day we will reunite with them in Heaven.

Prayer of Application

Almighty and loving God, You have created us out of love and continue to watch over us. You know what is best for us and our deceased loved ones. We might struggle to say goodbye to our departed loved ones now, but we feel content to entrust them into Your loving arms. All the wickedness of this world can tempt or harm them no more. We want to keep connecting with them and Your heavenly kingdom by trying to do as many good deeds every day as possible. That is how we can prepare ourselves to meet them again in Heaven someday.

Day Two: Fr. Peter Vu

Scripture: Romans 8:35, 38–39, NABRE

What will separate us from the love of Christ? Will anguish, or distress, or persecution, or famine, or nakedness, or peril, or the sword? . . . For I am convinced that neither death nor life, nor angels, nor principalities, nor present things, nor future things, nor powers, nor height, nor depth, nor any other creature will be able to separate us from the love of God in Christ Jesus our Lord.

Devotional Reading: "Voice of an Angel"

We need food and water to survive on earth. We also rely on love to give us strength and courage to overcome our daily challenges. We also know human love can be destroyed easily by all sorts of things, especially a tragedy. We Christians have a much more reliable source of love in Jesus to empower us on our faith journeys. Paul is the voice of an angel to remind us about that special love in the Scripture passage above. The loss of our loved one or a sad tragedy does not mean that Jesus loves us less and lets it happen to us without much concern. Like the love of a parent to a child, Jesus's love for us is not lessened a bit because of this sad event. He wants us to know that nothing can change His love for us. He will always love us and continue to help us overcome our current and future challenges.

Prayer of Application

Loving and faithful God, You have shown us Your love in your Son Jesus. You have saved us by sacrificing Your only Son on the cross. In this anguish and stressful time, we might feel that You have abandoned us or Jesus has stopped loving us. But Paul—an angel—shares with us the Scripture passage above to let us know that Jesus's love for us remains the same today, yesterday, and tomorrow. If we have ever felt discouraged or depressed because of this tragedy, we just need to look up to the cross of Jesus to remind us of His enduring love for us. His love will help us get through this tough time and conquer future challenges. Amen.

Day Three: Fr. Peter Vu

> ### *Scripture: Philippians 3:20–21, NABRE*

But, our citizenship is in Heaven, and from it we also wait for a savior, the Lord Jesus Christ. He will change our lowly body to conform with His glorified body by the power that enables Him also to bring all things into subjection to Himself.

Devotional Reading: "Word of Encouragement"

We all claim at least one country to be our home. A country that everyone loves to be their home is the United States of America. The reason for this is America gives its citizens all kinds of rights and opportunities. People risk their lives and face numerous dangers to come to America. But there is one place much better than America—namely, Heaven. We Christians love to claim our citizenship up there for after this life. In that new home, we will witness how Jesus would raise us up from the dead and bless us with eternal life. He will also put an end to death and be the judge of the living and the dead on the Last Day. The transition of our deceased loved ones from this life to the next might be tough for us to accept. However, they are claiming the best citizenship for themselves in Heaven. We are happy for them as they will enjoy many wonderful blessings in their new home.

Prayer of Application

Lord Jesus, Savior, and judge of the world, You have prepared for us the way to Heaven with Your cross and resurrection. You know that is the best home for us to enjoy eternal life and the other blessings that we cannot find in this life. We feel honored to claim our citizenship in Heaven. We realize that it breaks our hearts to say farewell to our deceased loved ones. But we know they are trading up their citizenship and going to be in a better home, to enjoy a new life. In Heaven, they will see no more suffering and death. They will have a new body and an eternal life to replace the old one. Paul wants to share with us those words of encouragement and the good news in the Scripture above during this time of grief. Hopefully, we can find comfort in those uplifting words and look up to Heaven as our home after this life whenever we remember our deceased loved ones. Amen.

Day Four: Fr. Peter Vu

> ### Scripture: *John 11:21–22, 25–26, NABRE*

Martha said to Jesus, "Lord, if you had been here, my brother would not have died. But, even now I know that whatever you ask God, God will give you." . . . Jesus told her, "I am the resurrection and the life; whoever believes in me, even if he/she dies, will live; and everyone who lives and believes in me will never die. Do you believe this?"

Devotional Reading: "Reassuring Spirit"

One of the special relationships we have in this life is the one between siblings. Martha only had a brother Lazarus and a sister Mary. They were a close-knit family and good friends with Jesus. Martha sent word to the Lord about Lazarus's serious health condition and wish for him to be healed. Unfortunately, he died before Jesus could heal him. Martha expressed her grief and disappointment with Jesus. He tried to reassure her about His divine power over this life and the next. Martha was convinced by Jesus's reassuring spirit and put her hope in him. Jesus ended up restoring Lazarus back to life. Our deceased loved ones might not be raised from the dead in this life. However, if we put our trust and hope in Jesus, we know they will experience the resurrection in the next life. As He did to Martha, Jesus comes to us today and asks, "Do you believe this?"

Prayer of Application

Jesus, friend of the broken and hope of the downtrodden, You restored Martha's spirit with Your presence and miracle as she mourned the loss of her brother. As we face the loss of our loved ones, we ask You to lift our spirits and restore our hope with Your peace and love. We believe that You will raise up our deceased loved ones and bless them with eternal life on the Last Day. Whenever we celebrate Easter, Your resurrection reassures us about that belief and strengthens our hope in eternal life. We look forward to each Easter to be reminded of Your promise for our deceased loved ones and feel reassured they are in Your good hands. Amen.

Day Five: Fr. Peter Vu

Scripture: John 14:1–3, 5–6, NABRE

Do not let your hearts be troubled. You have faith in God; have faith also in me. In my Father's house, there are many dwelling places. If there were not, would I have told you that I am going to prepare a place for you? And if I go and prepare a place for you, I will come back again and take you to myself, so that where I am you also may be . . . Thomas said to Him [Jesus], "Master, we do not know where you are going, how can we know the way?" Jesus said to him, "I am the way, the truth, and the life. No one comes to the Father except through me."

Devotional Reading: "God's Whisper"

If a welcoming or reunion gathering brings us smiles and a rejoicing spirit, a farewell party makes us cry and feel anguished. Evidently, that is how the early disciples felt after their master died and returned to Heaven. Knowing how they felt, Jesus tried to comfort them with the Scripture passage above and called on them to put their faith and hope in Him amid their uncertain future. For He will continue to show us the way to our home in Heaven and sustain our life on earth. The departure of our loved ones causes us a lot of anguish and pain. We do not want to say farewell to them, just like the early disciples did not want to depart with Jesus after His resurrection. Our Lord knows how we feel and wants to console us with the message above. He asks us to put our faith in Him and lets us know that he has already prepared a place in Heaven for our deceased loved ones. He also whispers this message in our ears: "I will come back again and take you to myself, so that where I am you also may be." We cannot wait for that day to be here so that we can see Him and reunite with our deceased loved ones in God's house.

Prayer of Application

Jesus, light and hope of the world, You comforted Your early disciples with the uplifting words in the Scripture passage above. You called on them to have faith in You and promised to prepare a place for them in God's house. As we grieve the loss of our loved ones, our Lord whispers in our ears His comforting words in the Scripture passage above and asks us to put our trust in Him.

He has prepared a place for them in God's house to enjoy eternal peace and happiness. Every time we look at our home here on earth, we are reminded of God's house in Heaven where our deceased loved ones are staying right now. We hope that our faith in Jesus will lead us there, to be reunited with them in Heaven someday. Amen.

Day Six: Katherine Brower

> ### Scripture: John 11:35, NRSV

Jesus began to weep.

Devotional Reading: "Tears"

Who has not felt the pain of loss? Who has not cried? Who has not wondered why there is a need for this kind of pain? Tears come in many forms. There are tears of joy. There are tears of loss. There are tears of laughter and tears of anger. What happens when there are no more tears and only emptiness? What can fill that void? Where can peace begin again? Sometimes, when we are emptied, our vision becomes clearer. That is when Christ, in his patience and compassion, comes to us in comfort and in peace. Jesus wept at the grave of Lazarus. He mourned the loss of one so dear to him. He brought Lazarus back to life in the same way we can be brought to life by opening ourselves to His love, His care, and His gifts of understanding and peace. But we must roll away the stone in front of us. We must be open to knowing the grave is not the end but a new beginning. We must weep and then see that Jesus is, in fact, with us in the pain, in the tears, and in the coming joy.

Prayer of Application

O God, whose Son is the good shepherd, help us to hear His voice, be comforted in knowing that wherever He leads us He will be with us. We pray that our tears may become tears of joy in the assurance of Christ's love and compassion for all. Amen.

Day Seven: Katherine Brower

> ### *Scripture: Hebrews 11:1, KJV*

Now faith is the substance of things hoped for, the evidence of things not seen.

Devotional Reading: "Faith"

What is faith? Where can we find it? Faith is the assurance of things hoped for, the conviction of things not seen. This definition of faith in the letter to the Hebrews can give us a starting point through our journey of grief. Our faith gives us hope. Hope is bound up with being alive. In the Bible, life and hope and being alive are intertwined. Life and hope and faith in God are intertwined in our looking forward to something good. We look forward to the coming glory. God is with us in our grief while helping us to see beyond our present day. Hope is necessary to our faith journey today and in the todays to come. Our faith gives us hope to hang on to our memories and assures us that God is with us in life and in death, in joy and in sorrow.

Prayer of Application

Almighty Father and ever-loving God, be with us today and for all of our tomorrows. You have made all things in Your wisdom and compassion. You, alone, know the boundaries of life and death. Help us to hear Your voice in this world and the world to come. Guide us in the understanding that through our confidence in Your love for us we may come to enjoy the rest and peace, which You have given to all in faith. We ask this through Jesus Christ who is Resurrection and Life, and who lives and reigns forever and ever. Amen.

Day Eight: Katherine Brower

> ### Scripture: John 3:16, NRSV

For God so loved the world that he gave his only Son, so that everyone who believes in him may not perish but may have eternal life.

Devotional Reading: "Enduring Love"

Bishop Desmond Tutu wrote, "If we have loved well while we were alive, there is life after death—our love will go on for generations." When we love, we have cared very deeply. Sometimes, that may make the loss of someone we loved even more painful. Our comfort through this pain is realizing and remembering the amazing and gracious love God has for us in our living and our dying. We can rest assured that we are loved. Our faith is a testament to this love. God loves us today and promises his love for all eternity. Our love for someone we grieve will not disappear. We are comforted that our love will go on for generations. God's love knows no boundaries.

Prayer of Application

Gracious and loving Father, You have taught us that without love, whatever we do has no worth. Let us see through Your love for us, which is our greatest gift, the true bond of peace and all virtue. We ask You to grant this through Your only Son, Jesus Christ, who lives and reigns with You and the Holy Spirit, one God, now and forever. Amen.

Day Nine: Katherine Brower

> ### Scripture: Romans 8:38–39, NRSV

For I am convinced that neither death, nor life, nor angels, nor rulers, nor things present, nor things to come, nor powers, nor height, nor depth, nor anything else in all creation, will be able to separate us from the love of God in Christ Jesus our Lord.

Devotional Reading: "Horizon of Faith"

I have a sympathy card to share whenever someone I know has suffered a loss. It is printed at a convent in Wisconsin. The words on the card can speak to us and remind us of a truth we know but may need to occasionally be reminded. They were written by Fr. Bede Jarrett, OP. His words are "Life is eternal and love is immortal, and death is only a horizon, and a horizon is nothing save the limit of our sight."

Our faith assures us there is life after death. But our vision while we are alive cannot allow us to see beyond our earthly horizons. We know it is there in the same way we know the sun will rise each morning in the east and set each evening in the west. We cannot see the sun before it rises, nor after it sets, but we know it is there just as we know that God's love and caring are there in our living and our dying. Nothing and no one can come between us and His love.

Prayer of Application

Father of all, we pray to You for those we love but see no longer. Grant them Your peace; let light perpetually shine upon them; and, in Your loving wisdom and almighty power, work in them the good purpose of Your perfect will, through Jesus Christ our Lord. Amen."[12]

Day Ten: Katherine Brower

Scripture: Psalm 27, NRSV

The Lord is my light and my salvation, whom shall I fear?

Devotional Reading: "Strength in Fear"

Rosa Parks once said she read the Psalms as a child and was comforted by the words in Psalm 27, to not be afraid. It may be why she is remembered for her strength in times when it would have been easy to be afraid. What do we have to fear in our journey through grief? Nothing. No one. Fear and sadness cannot overcome us. Jesus told us that those who mourn will be blessed. Our present loss may not feel like a blessing, but we are reminded through these words that we have been loved by God and have learned love through Him and that love never dies. Therein lies our blessing, not for just today but for all days. God is love. Love knows no boundaries.

Prayer of Application

Grant, O Lord, to all who are bereaved the spirit of faith and courage, that they may have the strength to meet the days to come with steadfastness and patience, not sorrowing as those without hope, but rather, in thankful remembrance of Your great goodness, reap the joyful expectation of eternal life with those they love. And this, we ask in the name of Jesus Christ, our Savior. Amen.

Day Eleven: Rev. Nancy Claus

> ### Scripture: Matthew 6:31–34, NABRE

Therefore, do not worry saying, "What shall we eat?" or "What shall we drink?" or "What shall we wear?" For your heavenly Father knows that you need all these things. But seek first the kingdom of God and His righteousness, and all these things shall be added to you. Therefore, do not worry about tomorrow, for tomorrow will worry about its own things. Sufficient for the day is its own trouble.

Devotional Reading: "The Divine Conductor of Our Lives"

Orchestras always amaze me! The fact that a conductor with a baton can guide the performance of an incredible number of instruments and players to produce such a harmonious symphony is truly remarkable. For the record, the actual number of musicians employed within a given performance may vary from seventy to more than 100. Yes, the orchestra is truly complex, but it produces such an amazing result—a symphony! When one watches and listens to an orchestra, it can be overwhelming to imagine the amount of work and preparation that goes into a single performance. It requires expertise and competence.

When God orchestrates by His divine power, He takes mankind by surprise. We can never understand the immenseness of His power over His creation. God is omnipotent and has at His command all the powers of the universe. All His works are done without effort. God's power is infinite and unlimited. God possesses what no creature can: an incomprehensible abundance of power and authority, which are absolute. This Divine Conductor is coordinating, arranging, planning, and organizing the various elements of our lives to produce the best results (quietly and in many instances, far ahead of time). God continues to orchestrate the world in which we live, and He wants to be the composer of your life.

You can trust God. He is big enough, knowledgeable enough, and loving enough to take care of you and your worries, no matter what you are going through. God isn't done with us. Trust Him.

When you wait upon the Lord to finish what He has started, you will remain in His presence for eternity. Do not be discouraged!

Prayer of Application

Lord God, You are eternal, faithful, and trustworthy. You are the Alpha and the Omega; you know the beginning from the end. You are always at work, faithfully hemming me in with abundant mercy and grace. Help me avoid worry. Thank you that I can trust You as I give all of my cares and fears to You. In Your holy name. Amen.

Day Twelve: Rev. Nancy Claus

> ### *Scripture: Ecclesiastes 12:13, NRSV*

Fear God and keep His commandments, for that is the whole duty of everyone.

Devotional Reading: "Forgetfulness"

In his classic novel, *One Hundred Years of Solitude,* Columbian author Gabriel Garcia Marquez tells of a village where people are afflicted with a strange plague of forgetfulness, a kind of contagious amnesia. The plague causes people to forget the names of even the most common, everyday objects. One young man, still unaffected, tries to limit the damage by putting labels on everything. "This is a table." "This is a window." "This is a cow; it has to be milked every morning." And at the entrance to the town, on the main road, he puts up two large signs. One reads, "The name of our village is Macondo," and the larger one reads, "God exists."

We all forget much of what we have learned in life. Much of our forgetting will do us relatively little harm. But if we forget to whom we belong, if we forget that our deepest longing is belonging to God, we may end up feeling like we are living in a world we scarcely understand.

In a God-aware relationship, however, our souls are ultimately satisfied in a meaningful life of goodness and grace, wholeness and holiness. The Book of Ecclesiastes very convincingly portrays the emptiness and confusion of life without a relationship with God. Every one of us has eternity in our hearts, and only Jesus can provide ultimate satisfaction, joy, and wisdom. Our highest good is found in the *One* who offers us abundant life.

Prayer of Application

Father, I pray You will help all of us impacted by the loss of a loved one to treasure being known and remembered by You. If we should forget You in our journey to life in the new heaven and earth, we will never outlive Your love and grace for us. The only things You are not going to remember are our sins. In Jesus's strong and loving name. Amen.

Day Thirteen: Rev. Nancy Claus

Scripture: Psalm 23: 1–3, NKJV

The LORD is my shepherd; I shall not want. He makes me lie down in green pastures. He leads me beside still waters.

He restores my soul. He leads me in paths of righteousness for
his name's sake. . .

Devotional Reading: "The 23rd Psalm"

For centuries the 23rd Psalm has been one of the most treasured passages in all of Holy Scripture. Its words are among the most comforting, often being quoted in times of trouble or distress. When the Good Shepherd speaks to His own, He never uses words of despair, hopelessness, frustration, defeat, discouragement, fear, confusion, or failure. Instead, He gives His sheep words of hope, rest, victory, peace, power, joy, triumph, and love.

David, the psalmist, has provided for us in the 23rd Psalm a word of hope that goes far beyond the limits of life into the shadows, which appear at times for every human being. Consider his carefully chosen description of death. Not a word was wasted as he pointed us to the only source of confidence in those especially difficult times in our lives.

He talked of his "walk *through* the valley of the shadow of death." He did not describe death in terms of a violent ocean, a stormy mountain, or a lifeless desert. He painted the image of a valley, that area at the foot of a peaceful mountain. David became a pioneer by defining the power of death by relegating it to only a shadow. The Lord was not only his Shepherd who supplied his needs but also his—and our—only source of light. Yet the most significant words in the 23rd Psalm are ones that we frequently read right over, without even giving much thought to the reassurance they offer. The psalmist spoke of a walk through the valley. It was not a walk *into* the valley. It was not a walk *in* the valley. It was not even a walk *around* the valley. Instead, the journey is *through* the valley. The length of the walk becomes insignificant once the discovery is made that the journey is only temporary. We can persevere as long as we can see the light.

Our walk is not a solo one. We have the best of company for our journey. A caring and loving shepherd, our Lord and Savior, will comfort us with His rod and His staff. Our Shepherd, Jesus Christ, does more than just tend to us; He laid down His life for us. He promises to carry you *through* the valley.

Prayer of Application

Dear Lord, it is a comfort to know that You are with me always; Your protection is unfailing and I do not need to fear because You hold me in the palm of Your hands. You will never let me go. In Your precious name. Amen.

Day Fourteen: Rev. Nancy Claus

> ### Scripture: 1 Chronicles 13:8, NKJV

Then David and all Israel played music before God with all their might, with singing, on harps, on stringed instruments, on tambourines, on cymbals, and with trumpets.

Devotional Reading: "The Gift of Music"

Music is one of God's greatest gifts to His people. It has the power to touch our hearts, lift our spirits, and bring us closer together and closer to God's glorious presence. The book of Psalms within Scripture is a collection of songs, and most of them were written by David. There are Psalms to fit every situation in our lives: psalms of praise, psalms of thanksgiving, psalms used at coronations of kings and queens, and psalms of lament—aimed toward individuals, nations, and worldwide audiences. There are psalms teaching wisdom, psalms of encouragement, and psalms that witness God's glory.

Can you imagine what life would be like without music?

Think about it for a moment: No bands or concerts or radio limited to stations airing the news, weather, and road conditions. Brides marching down aisles in silence. Our voices would not need a variety of tones; we would all talk in a monotonous way, like robots.

Can you imagine worship without music?

I guess we could still read scriptural lessons and the Psalms, responsively. We could pray. We would still have sermons and benedictions but without music. It just wouldn't be the same.

Music enriches our worship, and it enriches our lives.

During this time of sadness and grief, it is encouraging to note that songs of lament and praise have the power to lead us to tears. So, too, music has a way of piercing into the deep parts of our souls and assisting us in our expressions of sorrow and responses to God.

Music is a beautiful gift from God

Prayer of Application

Dear Lord, Just like hymnist, Walter E. Edmiaston, wrote in "There's a Song in My Heart I'm Singing Today," I sing as my prayer, "There's a song in my heart that is reigning today, so blessed, so holy and pure; Like a river it flows, and its blessing bestows, and in Christ evermore secure." With a joyful voice. Amen.

Day Fifteen: Rev. Nancy Claus

Scripture: Habakkuk 1:5, ESV

Look among the nations, and see; wonder and be astounded. For I am doing a work in your days that you would not believe if told.

Devotional Reading: "Working Overtime"

As we look at the entirety of our lives through the gracious lens of God's Providence, our hearts can be touched to know that Jesus has a design for us.

You may discover as you look back at your life, God designed some chapters to be long and delightful, others far too short, and some extremely painful. But we only see the meaning of our story when it fits into the context of the bigger, far greater story of Jesus Christ Himself. Surprisingly, the best of life's chapters are not always easy; they run deep when we are suffering and groping for the arms of our Savior.

The mysteries of God's Providence come into play in each of our lives, forcing us into uncharted and new directions. Our stories oftentimes turn out far different than originally planned. But that is the glorious part of God's mysterious ways!

If you are a follower of Jesus, every day of your life is weighted with Kingdom purpose, eternal significance, and a royal destiny filled with ultimate joy and contentment. Embrace the Lord's

Providence, for when it comes to endings, you cannot find a better author than the God of the Bible. Jesus has a design for your life and the lives of the ones whom you love. Only trust Him.

Prayer of Application

Dear Lord, thank you for the calm and quiet that You promise, accessible amid my fears and the uncertainty of life. Help me to remember that when I feel overwhelmed by what I cannot predict or plan, You already know the outcome. Enable me, Lord, to trust You as I steady my mind and heart on Your promises.

Day Sixteen: Rev. Nancy Claus

> ### Scripture: Psalm 91:9–12, NKJV

Because you have made the Lord, who is my refuge, even the Most High, your dwelling place. No evil shall befall you, nor shall any plague come near your dwelling. For He shall give His angels charge over you, to keep you in your ways. In their hands they shall bear you up, lest you dash your foot against a stone.

Devotional Reading: "Angels Among Us"[13]

Within the pages of a *Reader's Digest* magazine years ago, a writer shared the following true story. It is a powerful reminder that God uses His angels to protect and provide for us.

"A British Express Train raced through the night, its powerful headlight piercing the darkness. Queen Victoria of England was a passenger on the train. Suddenly the engineer saw a startling sight. Revealed in the beam of the engine's light was a strange figure in a black cloak standing in the middle of the tracks and waving its arms. The engineer grabbed for the brake and brought the train to a grinding halt.

He and his fellow trainmen jumped off the train to see what had stopped them. But they could find no trace of the strange figure. On a hunch, the engineer walked a few yards further up the tracks. Suddenly he stopped and stared into the fog in horror. The bridge had been washed out in the middle and ahead of them, the bridge had collapsed into the stream. If the engineer had not heeded the ghostly figure, his train would have plummeted down the stream.

While the bridge and the tracks were being repaired, the crew made a more intensive search for the strange flagman. But not until they got to London did they solve the mystery.

At the base of the engine's headlamp, the engineer discovered a huge moth. He looked at it a moment, then on impulse wet its wings and pasted it to the glass of the lamp.

Climbing back into the cab, he switched on the light and saw the 'flagman' in the beam. He knew the answer now: The moth had flown into the beam, seconds before the train was due to reach the washed-out bridge. In the fog, it appeared to be a phantom figure, waving its arms.

When Queen Victoria was told of the strange happening she said, 'I'm sure it was no accident. It was God's way of protecting us.'"

No, the figure the engineer saw in the headlight's beam was not an angel . . . yet God, quite possibly through the ministry of His unseen angels, had placed the moth on the headlight lens exactly when and where it was needed. Truly "For he (God) will command His angels concerning you to guard you in all your ways" (Psalm 91:11).

Prayer of Application

Thanks be to You, Lord God, our Creator and Sustainer, Lord of night and day. Sunset holds no fear for us, for You are there in the sunlight and in shadow. Lead us through the dawn into the light of a new day. Amen.

Day Seventeen: Rev. Nancy Claus

> ### Scripture: Isaiah 32:18, ESV

My people will abide in a peaceful habitation, in secure dwellings, and in quiet resting places.

Devotional Reading: "The Little Chapel That Stood"

Less than 100 yards from the entrance to the 9/11 Memorial Museum at Ground Zero in New York City, the Chapel of St. Paul stands. It was built in 1766. George Washington's family worshiped there. Alexander Hamilton's grave lies nearby. It has been a comfort to many. No one has ever been turned away from its doors. It has been an immigrant's refuge and a sojourner's gift of peace where hope is born and sorrows cease.

On 9/11, seven large buildings, including the twin towers were destroyed, but not the Chapel of St. Paul. It was and continues to be something of a wonder, a symbol of God's grace. As observed by an individual praying on her knees inside St. Paul's when the towers were hit, the chandeliers never swayed; no windows were broken, and no roof tiles moved out of place.

Immediately after the terrorist attack, St. Paul's doors opened wide to the rescue teams. The firemen who were not on duty immediately left their homes in the burrows, carrying their boots. They were instructed to meet at St. Paul's Chapel. They hung their shoes on its iron fence, booted up, and raced into the living Hell of chaos and casualty. Sadly, 343 firefighters never returned to St. Paul's to retrieve their shoes. So, too, sixty police officers and eight paramedics perished.

Many are astonished that the old St. Paul Chapel didn't collapse and burn on 9/11; still others are not surprised at all. Why? Because they know that the light which shines from the cross has always brought wonders into the darkness. The cross has always shone with the power to overcome and defeat the moral helplessness that has humanity in its grip. The light of the cross shines for the sick and the sinner—for all of us. Not all the darkness of evil in the world can extinguish that light.

Lean upon that glorious cross. It is a place where you can leave your worries, concerns, and fears.

Prayer of Application

Father, I pray that You will give me courage and peace as I face the unknown, just like the first responders did on that fateful day. Remind me of Your loving care and presence during times of worry and fear. In Your name, I pray. Amen.

Day Eighteen: Rev. Nancy Claus

Scripture: Philippians 4:6–7

Do not be anxious about anything, but in every situation, by prayer and petition, with thanksgiving, present your requests to God. And the peace of God, which transcends all understanding, will guard your hearts and your minds in Christ Jesus.

Devotional Reading: "Pure Joy"

"The Epistle of Philippians was written by Paul when he was in prison with iron shackles around his wrists; yet there is no iron in this book. It is full of light, love, and joy, blended with traces of sorrow, with a holy delight that rises above his grief."[14]

As Kay Warren, co-founder of Saddleback Church with Rick Warren, wrote, "Joy is the settled assurance that God is in control of all the details in our lives, the quiet confidence that ultimately everything is going to be all right, and the determined choice to praise God in every situation."[15]

"Rejoice in the Lord always," says Apostle Paul, "For joy is a most influential grace, and every child of God ought to possess it in a high degree."[16]

Worry can take joy completely out of your life. Did you know that 40 percent of the things most people worry about never happen? Thirty percent of our worries are related to past matters, which are now beyond our control. Twelve percent of our worries have to do with our health, even when we are not actually ill. Ten percent of our worries are about friends and neighbors and are not based on evidence or fact. Only 8 percent of our worries have some basis in reality, which means that 90 percent of the things we worry about will *never* happen![17]

There are times in all our lives when we feel distant from God—our loving, tender, unchangeable God. It is difficult to believe He remains right beside us and always will. And yes, sometimes it is difficult to rejoice. Maybe you are distracted by your own set of troubles, difficulties, and disappointments. Maybe you are experiencing poor health or diminished physical and cognitive ability. Maybe you are feeling lonely and you desperately possess the desire to belong, whether to someone or something.

The miracle of belonging is that whether we deserve it or not, whether we know it or not, whether we accept it or not, we belong to our Lord Jesus Christ. He has already given himself to us and for us. All we need to do is invite him into our hearts and accept His Lordship.

May you, this very day like the Apostle Paul, be humbly confident, patient, and with full assurance of faith that Jesus Christ is our only refuge and strength; our only hope and confidence. Rejoice in the Lord always. Again. I will say, Rejoice!

Prayer of Application

Thank you, Lord, for the promise that I am never alone. I often feel I am sinking or have been left adrift by friends and family; sometimes, there is no one to reach out to in human contact, to remind me that You are there for me in my pain. In this, I pray. Amen.

Day Nineteen: Rev. Nancy Claus

> ### *Scripture: 1 Peter 5:10*

And the God of all grace, who called you to his eternal glory in Christ, after you have suffered a little while, will himself restore you and make you strong, firm and steadfast.

Devotional Reading: "The Reason For Our Hope"

No word is more beautifully descriptive of the Gospel of Jesus Christ than hope, with its assurance, trust, and expectation. Hope is a gift. When it arrives, despair departs. It has been said that "hope pierces the darkness."

Christian hope is never merely wishful thinking or a consoling dream of our imagination; it is ever grounded on the divine act of salvation accomplished in Jesus Christ.

Paul refers to our inheritance as our unseen hope for which we wait with patience. He writes of the hope to which we have been called, the hope laid up for us in Heaven, our glorious hope, our good hope, and our hope of eternal life.

Even though the word *hope* appears in the Epistles of Paul over forty times, we search in vain for any full or detailed explanation as to why we experience times of difficulty, grief, and suffering. The New Testament offers few answers to many of the questions we wish we had, probably because such knowledge is beyond our finite comprehension. Maybe you or a loved one are longing for hope and cannot find it during this time of life. Please know, it is not a futuristic aspiration. It is yours for the taking. The Bible says that Jesus Christ is the very hope that lies within. He is earth's only hope. He came to unlock the door of your soul to bring the light of salvation into your life.

His compassions do fail not. They are new every morning; Great is His faithfulness (Lamentations 3:22–23).

Prayer of Application

Most merciful God, You hold each of us dear to Your heart. In that knowledge, assure me that my loved ones and I are not alone during this time of uncertainty. Give us courage and faith for all that is to come, for we know that You will always be by our side. It is in Your name, I pray. Amen.

Day Twenty: Mike Gruppen

> ### Scripture: Matthew 11:28–30

Come to me, all you who are weary and burdened, and I will give you rest. Take my yoke upon you and learn from me, for I am gentle and humble in heart, and you will find rest for your souls. For my yoke is easy and my burden is light.

Devotional Reading: "Heavy Lifting"

As a powerlifter, I have lifted a lot of heavy weights in my life. But nothing had prepared me for the heavy weight of grief that I experienced after losing my dad and my sister within weeks of each other. The extreme sadness and disappointment I experienced were crushing me, and I felt hopeless. How could this be? I am usually a strong person, there for everyone else. Yet for the first time in my life, I felt extremely weak and incapable of even facing the day. It was at this time that I came to a true understanding of God's offer of His strength, written about in the Book of Matthew.

I gave God my burdens each morning, and He was right there to lift the heavy weight of grief for me. God began to show me in a deeper way that He will tangibly take our burdens and hand us something back in return. When I hand Him my sadness, He hands me His comfort and reminds me of His love for me.

When I hand Him my feelings of aloneness, He hands me reminders that He will never leave me; He will provide for me and take care of me. I'm thankful for the way God's promises encourage my soul and bring some peace to my mind. It doesn't take the grief away, but it releases its heavy weight.

Prayer of Application

God, I come to You today and hand You my heavy burdens and weights, and I'm asking You to fill me with Your rest and peace for my mind and body. I trust that You are with me today and that You will help me through this difficult season. Help my eyes to recognize Your hand guiding me today, that I may feel You fill me with the Spirit.

Day Twenty-One: Mike Gruppen

> **Scripture: Philippians 4:6–7**

Do not be anxious about anything, but in every situation, by prayer and petition, with thanksgiving, present your requests to God. And the peace of God, which transcends all understanding, will guard your hearts and your minds in Christ Jesus.

Devotional Reading: Victory Over Grief

My journey with grief has been more intense than any other emotional journey I have dealt with. At times, the grief and pain seem all-consuming, and I feel that I am in a cloud of heaviness. My experience is that most other emotions are relatively short-lived. Unfortunately, grief tends to stick around and even "intensify" at unexpected times. I have heard it said that there is no expiration date on grief, and I can confirm this. At times grief can seem so overwhelming that you begin to wonder if you will ever experience joy again.

This verse has been a huge part of my victory over extreme grief. Reading this verse aloud and praying this over my life has truly brought "peace that passes all understanding" into my life. I still have hard days, but God's presence surrounds me with His peace and allows Joy to shine through into my memories. I have tangibly experienced God's strength and peace filling me when I did not feel I could even get out of bed. His mercy is new every morning and He has shown me that He is with me in these difficult days.

Prayer of Application

God, thank You that Your strength fills me when I am weak and that You show me You are with me every step on the path on this journey of grieving. Your word is true, and I choose to trust in Your promises that You will bring peace to my anxious mind. Help me to deepen my trust that You are with me.

Day Twenty-Two: Jenny Gruppen

> **Scripture: *John 10:10, ESV***

The thief comes to steal, kill and destroy but I have come to give you life and have it abundantly.

Devotional Reading: "God is with me"

One thing I have learned in my forty-eight years is life is hard and out of my control. My life hasn't turned out the way I dreamed it would. I lost my sweet little sister to leukemia at age fourteen. My parents divorced soon after, and I have seen cancer steal life way too early from several other family members. As a result of those losses, I experienced moments of deep sadness, anger at God, grief, loneliness, and, at times, wondered where God was and questioned why He wasn't listening to my prayers. I began deeply seeking God for answers, asking Him to speak to me.

Through that journey, God began to teach me some important truths that I am so grateful for now. He led me to John 10:10, the verse above. God showed me through that Scripture and several others that God is for us; He loves us and has good plans for our life, but our enemy, Satan, is the one who has come to steal life and try to destroy us emotionally. God began showing me that His promises in the Bible are true and that He desires for me to lean into Him, not allowing my circumstances to dictate what I think about Him. My anger toward God shifted away from God and moved to lean into His promises, allowing God to help my heart to heal and strengthen me in the journey of grief—still today.

Every day, I began to say out loud, "God is with me. God is for me, and He is here to help and strengthen me today."

Prayer of Application

God, thank You for Your love and strength that will get me through today. I choose to lean into Your promises and not follow my feelings, which are just based on my circumstances. Even though I feel alone, I know You are with me today, and You will fill me with the strength I need for each moment.

Day Twenty-Three: Jenny Gruppen

Scripture: John 14:27, ESV

Peace I leave with you; my peace I give to you. Not as the world gives do I give to you. Do not let your hearts be troubled and do not be afraid.

Devotional Reading: "But God"

Grief is a lonely place, one where it feels like no one understands the depth of pain I am feeling. Grief is painful; grief is tiring; grief is overwhelming, and at some moments, I don't see how I am going to make it through this. I have learned that the more I dwell on those feelings of pain, the worse I feel. My mind replays over and over how hard grief is, and then more pain overcomes me. God has been reminding me that He is with me and, even though I may feel this way, He is offering me His peace to grab ahold of today.

I felt alone, BUT GOD gave me . . .

Deuteronomy 31:6: "Be strong and courageous, do not be afraid or terrified because of them, for the Lord your God goes with you, he will never leave you or forsake you."

And Isaiah 41:10 says, "So do not fear, for I am with you; do not be dismayed for I am the Lord your God. I will strengthen you and help you. I will uphold you with my righteous right hand."

I felt overwhelmed, BUT GOD said . . .

Psalm 73:26: "My flesh and heart may fail but God is the strength of my of heart and my portion forever."

I felt anxious, BUT GOD said . . .

John 14:27: "My peace I leave with you, my peace I give to you, not as the world gives do I give to you. Do not let your hearts be troubled and do not be afraid."

And He gave me Philippians 4:6–7: "Do not be anxious about anything, but in everything with prayer and petition and thanksgiving present your requests to God. And the peace of God which transcends your understanding, will guard your heart and mind in Christ Jesus."

I practiced meditating on these verses any time I felt alone, scared, or anxious, and I saw how they began to calm my emotions and bring me more peace. I would read them out loud over and over, and they sank into my heart, becoming my reality. I wrote them on sticky notes and placed them around my house and in my car, and I read them aloud when I saw them. God's Word began calming my heart and my emotions and filling me with peace. There was truly a difference! I have learned that life is hard, but God is with me through it, and I will be okay—in time—as God heals my heart and brings me His peace.

Prayer of Application

God, thank You that You are my comforter, my peace, my hope, and my strength for today, especially when I feel weak. I know You are with me, and I choose to put my trust in You. May You help my heart to not be troubled nor afraid as I see Your hand lifting me and showing me that You are near.

Day Twenty-Four: Jenny Gruppen

Scripture: Isaiah 40:29–31, NIV

He gives strength to the weary
and increases the power of the weak.
Even youths grow tired and weary,
and young men stumble and fall;
but those who hope in the LORD
will renew their strength.
They will soar on wings like eagles;
they will run and not grow weary,
they will walk and not be faint.

Devotional Reading: "God is my Strength"

After the death of my best friend, my heart was breaking, and I felt so tired. I didn't feel like I had the energy to accomplish the things I needed to do, and my brain felt foggy. I just wanted to lay on the couch and fill the day with Netflix. Feeling very alone, I wondered who I could share my deepest thoughts with, who would be there for me, and who would help me through all this *hard*. Grief had made me feel weak, disappointed, and so very alone.

God began showing me that He would give me the strength I needed each day, and He would be the one that would be there for me every day. I began to cling to the verses in Isaiah above. He gives strength to the weary and increases power for the weak. That felt like me.

This verse became a powerful source of strength for me, and each morning, I closed my eyes and pictured God filling me with His strength. I would visualize God lifting me up and taking me soaring with Him.

Visualization is a powerful tool to practice amid deep grief. Sometimes, our thoughts of grief can keep us stuck in tormenting pain, and we might feel as if we can't break out of the cycle of these painful thoughts. Visualizing peaceful places can bring calm to our emotions and shift our thoughts away from the pain to places of peace.

My peaceful place is Lake Michigan, so I often picture myself sitting at the beach with God next to me, and my body begins to relax. I picture the waves, the sun, and the great memories I have in my heart. Then, peace floods my heart and mind. I am so thankful that "God is near to the broken-hearted and saves those who are crushed in their spirit" (Psalm 34:18).

Prayer of Application

God, thank You that You are near to the broken-hearted and save those who are crushed in their spirits. I need Your strengthening today, and I'm asking You to fill me anew with Your peace. My heart is troubled, but I choose not to fear but rather to put my trust in You. I know that Your peace is enough for today, and Your strength is enough for each minute. Fill me up, God!

Day Twenty-Five: Pastor George Davis

Scripture: Psalm 46:1

God is our refuge and strength, an ever present help in trouble.

Devotional Reading: "Who Can We Run To; Where Can We Turn?"

The loss is great. You can't sleep or eat. You stay up all night wondering *why*. When the days are long, and you desire the pain to be gone . . . when life's interruptions, those significant emotional events paired with despair, cause you to question, *where is God?*

It's in those times we can run to and turn to God. Why? Because Scripture is clear: God is the creator, giver, and sustainer of all things,

God, *Jehovah Jireh*, the provider of all things, comforts us as He promises to be a refuge, a hiding place in times of trouble. When the tears of our tragedies and the torment and turmoil of our situations overflow our emotional banks, like a flood, He is an ever-present, all-encompassing help. Who can we run to? Where can we turn? What can we do?

We can on stand on God's promise to always be there. We can trust Him to protect us in all that we go through. And we can rest in God's surpassing peace. Because He has proclaimed that He is our refuge and strength.

Prayer of Application

Father God, in times of trouble and despair, please remind us that You are our refuge and strength. As You promise to always be with us, please help us to feel Your presence with every breath we take. Through my pain, I will commit to praise and worship You. Have mercy on me, Jesus, and help ease my suffering. Amen.

Day Twenty Six: Pastor Josh Baron

> **Scripture: *John 21:1–3*, NLT**

Afterward Jesus appeared again to his disciples, by the Sea of Galilee. It happened this way: Simon Peter, Thomas (also known as Didymus), Nathanael from Cana in Galilee, the sons of Zebedee, and two other disciples were together. "I'm going out to fish," Simon Peter told them, and they said, "We'll go with you." So they went out and got into the boat, but that night they caught nothing.

Devotional Reading: "The Numbness of Grief"

When someone close to us dies, it can come as a complete and utter shock. Our world might feel like it has shattered into a million pieces, and we are left bewildered and confused about what has happened. "How can this be?" we wonder. And when the initial shock starts to wear off, the horror of reality sets in. We find ourselves longing for the way things used to be. The shock, confusion, and longing create a numbing effect that makes it difficult to grieve outwardly because it is hard to put our finger on what exactly it is we are feeling. We shut down. We go numb.

The disciples may have experienced this part of grief in the aftermath of Jesus's death. Sure, Jesus appeared to them several times after the resurrection, but the story in John 21 gives the impression that the roller-coaster ride of Jesus appearing and then disappearing again was making Peter long for the way things used to be. When he says, "I'm going out to fish," you can almost hear him say, "I can't take this anymore! Maybe I'm not cut out for this challenge. I want to go back to the way things used to be." Remember, before Peter was a disciple of Jesus, he was a fisherman. The good news is that if you read a little further into the story, Jesus appears to the disciples again, calls to them, feeds them, and restores them. In the shock and numbness of your grief, pay attention to the mysterious ways through which Jesus appears to you, calls to you, feeds you, and restores you.

Prayer of Application

God, You come to us in our darkest hour, when we feel numb to the pain that we suffer. Awaken our senses so we can hear Your voice calling to us and taste the sweetness of Your grace that sustains us—which is sufficient for all of our needs. Amen.

Day Twenty-Seven: Pastor Josh Baron

Scripture: John 4:15

The woman said to him, "Sir, give me this water so that I won't get thirsty and have to keep coming here to draw water."

Devotional Reading: "The Yearning of Grief"

Losing someone we love leaves a painful void that we suddenly don't know what to do with. The person who we used to count on to fill that void is gone, and now, we have no one to comfort us in our agony. We always envisioned our future would involve our loved ones, but these expectations we had for our life are now also gone. Our hearts, souls, and bodies yearn to have the void filled by the person we've lost.

The Samaritan woman who Jesus met at the well was well acquainted with the yearning of grief. We don't know the exact circumstances that contributed to the woman's situation, but it is safe to assume that anyone who has had seven different spouses will have gone through significant loss and grief, whether the loss of relationship came through divorce or death. Jesus recognizes that she is yearning to fill the void in her life by looking for love wherever she can find it and offers her the kind of life that will quench her thirst.

As you go through the yearning stage of grief, acknowledge that these feelings and the desire to connect relationally are a natural stage of grief. Process these feelings by talking about them with a trusted friend. If you don't work through this stage of the grieving process, you may spend much of your life trying to replace what you've lost.

Prayer of Application

Triune God, You exist in community and have created us to be in relationship with You and others. In our yearning for connection, may we discover that You are the ultimate desire of our hearts. Put people in our path who will know how to love us and care for us in our grief, in ways that reveal Your love. Amen.

Day Twenty-Eight: Pastor Josh Baron

Scripture: 1 Kings 19:3–5

Elijah was afraid and ran for his life. When he came to Beersheba in Judah, he left his servant there, while he himself went a day's journey into the wilderness. He came to a broom bush, sat down under it and prayed that he might die. "I have had enough, Lord," he said. "Take my life; I am no better than my ancestors." Then he lay down under the bush and fell asleep.

Devotional Reading: "The Despair of Grief"

Elijah was in the depths of despair when he received the life-threatening message from Queen Jezebel in 1 Kings. What does despair sound and look like? We ask "why," feel angry and believe that we've been treated unfairly, think that our life will never be worth living again, and are ready to give up. Depression might sink in, and we find it difficult to get out of bed and end up sleeping most of the day.

If we don't work through our despair, we may go through life feeling angry at the world, others, and ourselves. If left unresolved, we could develop a negative attitude toward life and simply give up on experiencing joy, purpose, and fulfillment.

Thankfully, when Elijah was in the depths of despair and ready to give up on life, God sent an angel who spoke to Elijah and provided him food for the journey ahead. You'll need God to nourish you for the journey ahead because, as with Elijah, the journey will be too hard for you too. Look to see who God is sending you to show care in your grief and despair. What are the different ways in which God is nourishing you and strengthening you at this time so you can continue this journey?

Prayer of Application

Jesus, the Bread of Life, give us the strength we need today to meet the challenges of our grief. Where there is despair in our hearts, nourish us with Your words of hope and encourage us with Your angels and saints. Amen.

Day Twenty-Nine: Pastor Josh Baron

> ### Scripture: Job 42:12–17

The Lord blessed the latter part of Job's life more than the former part. He had fourteen thousand sheep, six thousand camels, a thousand yoke of oxen and a thousand donkeys. And he also had seven sons and three daughters. The first daughter he named Jemimah, the second Keziah and the third Keren-Happuch. Nowhere in all the land were there found women as beautiful as Job's daughters, and their father granted them an inheritance along with their brothers. After this, Job lived a hundred and forty years; he saw his children and their children to the fourth generation. And so Job died, an old man and full of years.

Devotional Reading: New Beginnings

Of the many losses Job suffered, the most terrible was the loss of his children. Job grieves by tearing his clothes, shaving his head, and lamenting to God. Job's grief was complicated because his friends and wife were not particularly supportive or comforting. But Job journeyed his way through grief, which culminated in his encounter with the wildness of God, and in the whirlwind of his acceptance of the truth, learned he has very little control in life. After Job's encounter with God, he not only recovered his livestock two-fold but also had ten more children.

While these were great blessings to Job, they alone don't demonstrate that Job was coming out of the dark tunnel of grief. Simply replacing things or people we've lost with other things or different people doesn't bring healing. However, if you pay attention to the names Job gives to his three new daughters, you'll see a significant change has taken place in Job's heart. If you look these names up in a Hebrew dictionary, you'll find they are difficult to translate. Some scholars suggest the best translations for these unusual and seemingly nonsensical names are *dove, perfume,* and *eyeshadow.*

What might this say about Job's transformation through the grief process? Perhaps the carefree and whimsical naming of his daughters is a sign that as he makes a new beginning in life, he isn't going to take the fragility and wildness of life for granted; he's not going to take life "too seriously." A new way of life has emerged, teaching Job that since nothing in life is guaranteed, he will try to live the rest of his days with joy and laughter.

Prayer of Application

Lord over life and death, it is You who hold all things together. And it is You who holds me together right now. Although I may feel more comfortable thinking I am in control of my life and what happens, that control is an illusion. Help me to let go of the need to control. Thank You that You became human so that I didn't have to pretend to be God. Help me to trust in Your goodness so I can laugh with joy again. Amen.

Day Thirty: Pastor Josh Baron

> ### Scripture: Revelation 22:1–5

Then the angel showed me the river of the water of life, as clear as crystal, flowing from the throne of God and of the Lamb down the middle of the great street of the city. On each side of the river stood the tree of life, bearing twelve crops of fruit, yielding its fruit every month. And the leaves of the tree are for the healing of the nations. No longer will there be any curse. The throne of God and of the Lamb will be in the city, and his servants will serve him. They will see his face, and his name will be on their foreheads. There will be no more night. They will not need the light of a lamp or the light of the sun, for the Lord God will give them light. And they will reign for ever and ever.

Devotional Reading: "Living and Trusting Again"

You have been through so much to make it to this point in the grieving process. And while everyone grieves differently and according to their own timetables, it is a step-by-step process for everyone. It is much like how we follow Jesus as disciples, one step at a time. Just as trust is a necessary ingredient in our following after Jesus, trust is also something that grows in us as we heal through the grieving process. The wonderful promise that Revelation 22 offers us is that wherever Jesus (who is the water of life) goes, life and growth and healing thrive! How can you hold on to this promise today as you continue to trust and follow Jesus? How do you see your trust in God growing as you continue to heal?

Prayer of Application

Jesus, Light of the world, thank You for how You have lit my path during the dark days of my grief journey. Jesus, water of life, thank You for bringing forth tender green shoots of new life from the stumps of my pain and loss. Growth and healing are good but can be painful and scary too. Help me to continue following You, trusting that wherever You go, there will be life to the full. Amen.

About The Contributors

The Grief Sojourners

Jill Plasman, HR business partner, JP HR Consulting

Gerilyn May, Faith Hospice employee, president of ELE! Everybody Love Everybody! Foundation, and Stephen's mom

Carl Paganelli, NFL official, Faith Hospice ambassador

Dianne Reed, Faith Hospice volunteer, Holland Home Foundation Board member

Jolynn VanWienen, founder and executive director, Starlight Ministries, Hudsonville, Michigan

Sandi Veenkamp, Faith Hospice family, Faith Hospice volunteer

Laura Alley Hoekstra, Faith Hospice family, End-of-life doula

Allison Moores, teenage author of *Murderer's Blade*

Cynthia Kay, business owner, speaker, author of *Small Business For Big Thinkers* and *Stop Wishing. Stop Whining. Start Leading*

Jennifer Feurestein, associate state director, AARP Michigan

Buck Matthews, retired radio and television personality, author of *Getting Here*

Ann Webb, vice president of Treatment Services KPEP

Paula Jauch, speaker, podcaster, award-winning author of *Cross Addicted: Breaking Free From Family Trauma And Addiction*

Kimberly M. Johnson, artist, author of *Holland's Big Red: My Happy Place*

Les Beimers, Holland Home resident, Raybrook campus

Danielle Josephine DeWitt, senior foundation specialist for Donor Relations and Stewardship, Spectrum Health Foundation, Helen DeVos Children's Hospital Foundation

Steve Kelly, radio host for WOOD Radio Morning Show

Nancy Poland, author of *Dancing With Lewy: A Father Daughter Dance Before and After Lewy Body Dementia Came to Live With Us.*

Vonnie Woodrick, founder iunderstand love heals, author of *i understand: Pain, Love and Healing after Suicide*

Jeff Elhart, Playground Director II Elhart Automotive Campus; co-author of *be nice. Four Simple Steps To Recognize Depression and Prevent Suicide*

Janet V. Grillo, author of *God Promised Me Wings To Fly; Life for Survivors after Suicide*

David Morris, PhD, author of *Lost Faith* and *Wandering Souls*, publisher of Lake Drive Books, literary agent at Hyponymous Consulting

Scott Winters, Grand Rapids radio personality, 98.7 WFGR

The Devotional Pastors

Father Peter Vu, pastor, St. Mary Magdalene Catholic Church, Kentwood, Michigan, chaplain, Grand Rapids Home for Veterans, and author, *Living For A Higher Purpose* and *Lord Jesus, I Want To See*

Reverend Katherine Brower, retired deacon, Episcopal Diocese of Western Michigan

Reverend George Davis, pastor, From the Heart Christian Community Church, Grand Rapids, Michigan

Reverend Nancy Claus, ordained minister, Reformed Church of America

Mike Gruppen, The Conqueror International Strength Team

Jenny Gruppen, Faith Hospice grief counselor

Reverend Josh Baron, LMSW, MDiv, director of Chaplaincy and Social Services at Raybrook of Holland Home

About The Authors

As a television meteorologist, Terri DeBoer has delivered West Michigan's "wake up" weather for three decades. Terri also co-hosts a daily lifestyle show eightWest. Her first book, *Brighter Skies Ahead: Forecasting A Full Life When You Empty The Nest*, outlines the journey parents go on as they "empty the nest"—a season filled with melancholy and loneliness, sometimes guilt and

regret. This "emptying the nest" transition is very much a journey of grief and sparked the creative idea to team up with Janet Jaymin to write this book about the universal truth that every human will experience at least one journey of grief. Terri resides in Byron Center, Michigan. Connect with Terri at www.terrideboer.com.

Co-author Janet Jaymin holds a Master's Degree in Counseling from Western Michigan University, and she is a National Board Certified counselor, Licensed Professional Counselor, and Certified Grief Counselor. Janet is a member of the Faith Hospice leadership team and a member of several hospice associations that include

National Association for Homecare & Hospice, National Hospice & Palliative Care Organization, and the Michigan Homecare & Hospice Association. Janet has provided content for Advice for Life through the *Grand Rapids Press* on various topics of grief, such as "Many ways to support a friend who is grieving" and "A Survival Guide: Grief and the Holidays." She has given presentations on grief and loss to West Michigan retirement communities and been a contributor to the *Faith Hospice Mind Body & Spirit Magazine*. Janet has helped thousands of individuals and families process their feelings of loss while being present with them. She is a strong advocate for wanting those who are grieving, to "Grieve Well" and was the visionary who inspired the creation of the new Grief Support Center for Faith Hospice at Trillium Woods. Janet resides in Grand Rapids, Michigan.

Endnotes

1   The World Counts, accessed 07 March 2022, https://www.theworldcounts.com/populations/world/deaths.

2   Centers for Disease Control and Prevention, Deaths and mortality statistics, accessed 18 March 2022, https://www.cdc.gov/nchs/fastats/deaths.htm.

3   Shannon Sabo and Sandra Johnson, "Pandemic Disrupted Historical Mortality Patterns, Caused Largest Jump in Deaths in 100 Years," accessed 18 April 2022, https://www.census.gov>library>stories 2022/03.

4   American Psychological Association, "Grief," https://dictionary.apa.org/grief.

5   Terri DeBoer, *Brighter Skies Ahead: Forecasting A Full Life When You Empty The Nest,* (New York: Morgan James Publishing, 2021), 187.

6   https://m.facebook.com>drleaf

7   https://www.youtube.com/watch?v=kYWlCGbbDGI

8   https://www.youtube.com/watch?v=khkJkR-ipfw

9   Kubler-Ross, Elisabeth and Kessler, David. On Grief and Grieving Finding the Meaning of Grief Through the Five Stages of Loss. Scribner, 2005. Pg. 7

10   i understand love heals, https://www.iunderstandloveheals.org/who-we-are/.

11   Be nice, https://www.benice.org/.

12 Episcopal Church. The Book of Common Prayer and Administration of the Sacraments and Other Rites and Ceremonies of the Church : Together with the Psalter or Psalms of David According to the Use of the Episcopal Church. New York :Seabury Press, 1979.

13 Many of Rev. Nancy Claus's devotions are compilations of past sermons she has heard, read, or given. Where able—with the aid of internet research, notes, and/or memory—we have referenced some of the information and quotes. In other places, authors or sources are unknown.

14 C.H. Spurgeon, Exposition of Philippians, Precept Austin, accessed 22 March 2022, https://www.preceptaustin.org/spurgeon_on_philippians1.

15 Kay Warren, *Choose Joy: Because Happiness Isn't Enough*, (Ada, Michigan: Revell, 2012).

16 "Joy, A Duty," The Charles Spurgeon Sermon Collection, accessed 22 March 2022, https://www.thekingdomcollective.com/spurgeon/sermon/2405/.

17 Earl Nightingale. "The Fog of Worry (Only 8% of Worries are Worth It)," Nightingale Conant, 2021, accessed 22 March 2022, https://www.nightingale.com/articles/the-fog-of-worry-only-8-of-worries-are-worth-it/.

CPSIA information can be obtained
at www.ICGtesting.com
Printed in the USA
JSHW021048210123
36634JS00001B/19